개정판

나는 레스토랑 영어다

I'm Restaurant English

Reading, Dialogues 내용
MP3 파일 다운로드
www.kimoonsa.co.kr

기문사
www.kimoonsa.co.kr

책을 펴내면서

'글로벌'이란 단어가 우리의 일상이 된 국제화 시대에 호텔리어나 호텔의 레스토랑 전문 종사자로서 손님들에게 당당하고 자신있게 영어로 서비스를 할 수 있다는 것은 참으로 가슴 뿌듯한 일입니다. 외국인 고객을 접해야 하는 호텔전문 요원에게 영어는 필수적인 요건입니다. 레스토랑 서비스 영어로 단단히 무장이 된 인재라면 세계를 향해 경쟁력있게 적극적으로 나아갈 수 있을 것입니다. "나는 레스토랑 영어다"는 제목 그대로 레스토랑의 예약부터 시작하여 손님을 맞이하여 식음료를 서비스하고 계산을 마친 후 배웅할 때까지의 살아있는 영어표현을 확실히 습득하게 하는 것이 목표입니다.

"나는 레스토랑 영어다(I'm Restaurant English)**"**의 구성과 특징은 다음과 같습니다.

이 책은 레스토랑 예약부터 환송까지 고객과 레스토랑 전문요원의 동선을 따라 시간 순서로 세 개의 Chapter와 11개의 Unit으로 구성되었으며, 각 Unit에는 기본 **Reading, Vocabulary, Key Expressions, Dialogues, Grammar, Restaurant English Tips, Review& Exercises, Restaurant Quiz** 등 레스토랑 전문 영어 학습을 유익하면서도 재미있게 할 수 있도록 구성하였습니다. 각 Unit에서 Reading과 Dialogues 부분은 원어민들의 자연스런 실제 발화 속도로 녹음되어 있으므로 호텔전문인이 되기 위한 학생들의 영어 듣기 실력과 유창한 말하기 실력에 도움이 될 것입니다.

Chapter 1은 레스토랑을 이용하고자 하는 고객의 전화예약부터 레스토랑에 맞이하는 과정을 다루고 있으며, Chapter 2는 구체적인 레스토랑 안에서의 식사 및 음료서비스에 필요한 영어회화 표현을 중심으로 아침 식사 주문, 점심 식사 주문, 저녁 식사 주문 및 음료와 디저트 주문에 이르기까지 레스토랑의 자세한 서비스 업무에 초점을 맞추어 다양한 상황의 대화문을 실었습니다. Chapter 3는 레스토랑 서비스 영어를 보다 완벽하게 수행하기 위해 구성한 부분으로서 고객이 계산을 하고 레스토랑을 떠날 때까지의 영어와, 서비스 과정에서 생길 수 있는 불만사항을 해결하는 상황과, 호텔 숙박 고객을 위한 룸서비스 관련 학습도 할 수 있습니다. 마지막 11단원은 이 교재의 하이라이트이자 꽃이라고 할 수 있는 부분으로 레스토랑 서비스 실제 상황의 시간적 흐름 그대로 손님을 맞이하여 서비스 후 배웅하기까지의 일련 과정에서 반드시 숙지하여야 할 영어표현들을 총정리하고 있습니다.

Appendix에서는 호텔리어 및 호텔전문요원의 꿈을 가진 학생들의 취업 면접에 도움이 되도록 영어인터뷰 내용들을 풍부히 실었습니다. 면접질문에 자주 나오는 가치관과 관련된 여러 유명 인사들의 좌우명들과 함께 호텔리어를 위한 영어면접의 예시 및 레스토랑 서비스에서 필수적으로 알아야 용어들까지 소개하고 있습니다.

이 교재에서 저자는 어려운 영어표현보다는 레스토랑이라는 현장 감각과 생활 감각이 맞아 떨어질 수 있는, 간단하면서도 정확한 표현들을 사용하려고 많은 노력을 기울였습니다. 특히 현재 우리나라 교육 정책의 기본이 되어있는 국가직무능력기준(NCS)을 기반으로 한 교재를 염두에 두고서 호텔레스토랑 서비스 영어에 집중 조명을 하였습니다. 호텔레스토랑 서비스라는 능력단위와 그 하위 범주인 능력단위 요소들인 고객 예약 응대하기, 고객 영접하기, 메뉴 추천하기, 메뉴 주문받기, 음식 서빙하기, 고객 환송하기 등은 그 수행준거들과 함께 정확히 본 교재의 구성과 일치함을 밝힙니다.

마지막으로, 이 책이 호텔리어나 호텔 레스토랑 전문 서비스 요원이 되고자 하는 독자들의 소망에 조금이라도 보탬이 되기를 진심으로 바랍니다. 이 책의 출판을 흔쾌히 허락해 주신 기문사 대표님께 감사드리고, 책 표지를 정성껏 단장해 준 미술 전공의 남편과, 늘 바쁜 엄마를 이해하고 사랑으로 응원하며 영어교육 전문가로서의 조언도 아끼지 않는 나의 딸 미선과, 나의 든든한 아들 재문에게도 사랑과 고마움을 전하고 싶습니다.

2019년 2월

관악산 기슭에서

한 선 희

차 례 C·o·n·t·e·n·t·s

Chapter 1 Reservation & Greeting

Unit 1 Telephone Reservation 9
Unit 2 Changing, Confirming & Cancelling the Reservation 27
Unit 3 Welcoming & Seating the Guest 43

Chapter 2 Order Taking & Meal Services

Unit 4 Breakfast 65
Unit 5 Lunch 85
Unit 6 Dinner 101
Unit 7 Beverage & Dessert 121

Chapter 3 More on Restaurant Services

Unit 8 Handling Complaints 145
Unit 9 Paying the Bill & Goodbye 161
Unit 10 Room Services 175
Unit 11 All-in-One Expressions of Restaurant Service
(레스토랑 서비스영어 종합편) 191

Appendix

1. English Interview 203
2. 유명인사들의 좌우명 213
3. An Interview Model for a Hotel Clerk 215
4. Food & Beverage Terms 218

■ Answers 229

Chapter 1

Reservation & Greeting

나는
레스토랑 영어다

Telephone Reservation

Unit 1

Telephone Reservation

Unit 1

Telephone Reservation

Preview : Reading

▣ Food and Beverage

One of the most important incomes of the hotel is from the sales of food and beverage. The restaurant must create an enjoyable and relaxed atmosphere for all guests. The guests should enjoy their meals and drinks in the most comfortable way. Every restaurant personnel must be courteous, helpful, sales-minded, and fast in service. They should know the menu in detail and make it a daily habit to check the special of the day.

▣ Key Words

F&B(Food and Beverage)	음식과 음료	personnel	요원, 인사
income	수입	courteous	예의바른
create	창조하다	helpful	도움되는
relaxed	편안한	sales-minded	판매에 신경쓰는

atmosphere	분위기	in detail	상세히
comfortable	안락한	make it a habit to~	-를 습관같이 하다

▣ Reading Helper

1. 식음료 판매: 가장 중요한 호텔 소득 중 하나
2. 즐겁고 안락한 분위기
3. 레스토랑 요원 : 예의바르고 도움주고, 판매에 신경 쓰고, 신속한 서비스, 상세한 메뉴 지식, 당일의 특별메뉴를 매일 확인하는 것을 습관화해야 한다.

▣ Review of the Reading

1. 호텔의 가장 중요한 수입 the most important i__________ of the hotel
2. 식음료 food and b__________
3. 레스토랑 요원 restaurant p__________
4. 안락한 분위기 comfortable a__________
5. 정중하고, 도움이 되며, 판매에 신경쓰고, 서비스가 빠른 c__________, helpful, s__________ and fast in service
6. 상세한 메뉴지식이 있어야 should know the menu __________ detail
7. ~하는 것을 습관화해야 make __________ a habit __________ ~

Basic Vocabulary

▣ Fill in the blank with the meaning in Korean.

reserve		fully booked	
make a reservation		available	

party	non-smoking section
hold on	prefer

▣ Fill in each blank with a suitable word from the table above.

1. I'd like to ____________ a table for two.
2. I'm sorry, but we're ________________.
3. How many in your ______________?
4. Please book a table by the window ________________________.

Key Expressions

▣ Make a full sentence using the words given in the bracket.

1. 점심시간은 몇 시까지입니까?
(What, lunch, for, you, time, are, open, ?)

____

2. 내일 저녁 테이블을 예약하고 싶습니다.
(I'd, evening, for, like, reserve, to, a table, tomorrow)

____

3. 창가 쪽에 한 테이블이 남아 있습니다.
(window, the, table, there, one, is, left, by)

____

4. 성함과 전화번호가 어떻게 되십니까?
(number, may, have, name, phone, please, I, your, and, ?)

____

5. 정말 죄송합니다만 예약이 모두 완료되었습니다.
(I'm, booked, but, fully, sorry, really, we're)

____

6. 제가 해 드릴 다른 일이 있습니까?
(there, else, can, for, is, anything, I, do, you, ?)

____

7. 일행이 몇 분이십니까?
(party, how, persons, your, many, in, ?)

____

8. 어떤 이름으로 예약을 해드릴까요?
(a reservation, in, what, make, shall, I, name, ?)

____

9. 몇 시로 생각하고 계십니까?
(time, you, in, mind, have, do, what, ?)

____

10. 무엇을 도와드릴까요?

(you, do, what, I, can, for, ?)

Dialogues

Dialogue 1

R : Receptionist G : Guest

R The Mona Lisa Restaurant. May I help you?

G Yes. What time are you open for lunch?

R From 12 to 4, sir.

G Can I reserve a table for two at 1 o'clock?

R Hold on please. Let me see. Is it for today?

G Yes, it is.

R OK. There is one table left by the window. Would you like that?

G Sure. That's perfect.

Notes

♠ May I help you?
= How may I help you?
= What can I do for you?

♠ What time are you open for lunch? 점심시간은 몇시부터입니까?
= When do you open for lunch?

♠ From 12 to 4 12시부터 4시까지

♠ Hold on please. (끊지 말고 기다리세요)

♠ There is one table left by the window.
available
free

Dialogue 2

R: Receptionist G: Guest

R Four Seasons Restaurant. May I help you?

G Yes, please. What time do you open this evening?

R **At 5:00** every evening except Wednesday, sir. And we close at 11:00 p.m.

G **I'd like to reserve a table** for three tonight, please.

R For what time, sir?

G Around 8:00.

R **May I have your name, please?**

G David Johnson.

R A table for three at 8:00 tonight for Mr. Johnson.

G That's right.

R Thank you for calling us. Have a good day, sir.

G Thank you, good bye.

Notes

♠ At 5:00 at : 기간의 시점을 나타냄. I have lunch at noon.

♠ I'd like to reserve a table.
make a reservation

I'd like to ~ 하고 싶다. I want to 나 I wish to 보다 더 부드러운 표현

♠ May I have your name? 정중하게 이름을 물을 때

Dialogue 3

R : Receptionist G : Guest

R Good evening, Green Restaurant. How may I help you?

G I would like to make a reservation.

R What day do you want to come in?

G This Thursday at 6:00 p.m.

R **How many in your party?**

G Five.

R We have a table at 6:30. Will that be possible?

G Yes.

R **May I have your name and phone number?**

G John Brown. 010-9876-5432.

R Mr. Brown. **You have reserved a table on Thursday at 6:30 for a party of 5. Is there anything else I can do for you?**

G That will be all.

R Thank you for calling.

G Good bye.

Notes

♠ How many in your party? 일행이 몇 분이십니까?
= How many persons in your party?
= How many persons are there in your group?

♠ on Thursday at 6:30 for a party of 5. (요일 앞에는 on, 시각 앞에는 at)

♠ May I have your name and phone number? 성함과 전화번호가 어떻게 되세요?

♠ Is there anything else I can do for you? 그밖에 또 도와드릴 것이 있을까요?

Dialogue 4

R : Receptionist G : Guest

R Good evening. The Victor Cafe.

G Good evening. **I'd like to reserve a table for tomorrow evening.** When does your restaurant open?

R Dinner is from 6:00 p.m. to 10 p.m.

G Can I reserve a table for tomorrow evening?

R Of course, ma'am. May I have your name?

G Sunny Kim.

R Okay Ms. Kim. What time should we expect you?

G We'll be there at around 7:00.

R How many in your party?

G Four.

R All right. We'll reserve a table for four tomorrow evening at 7:00.

G Thanks a lot.

R Thank you, ma'am. **We'll be expecting you.**

Notes

- I'd like to reserve a table for tomorrow evening. 내일 저녁 테이블을 예약하고 싶습니다.
- We'll be expecting you. (오시기를 기대하고 있겠습니다)

Dialogue 5

R: Receptionist G: Guest

R The Riverside Restaurant. **Can I help you?**

G I'd like to make a reservation for this evening at 7:30.

R **For how many persons,** sir?

G For six, please.

R Who's making the reservation?

G Mr. Robert.

R OK. Mr. Robert, a table for six at 7:30.

G That's right.

R Thank you for calling us. I will see you this evening. Good bye, Mr. Robert.

G Thanks, bye.

Notes

♠ Can I help you?
 = May I help you?
 = What can I do for you?
 = Is there anything I can do for you? 무엇을 도와드릴까요?

♠ For how many persons? (몇 분이시죠?)

Dialogue 6

R: Receptionist G: Guest

R Barney Restaurant. What can I do for you?

G Yes, I'd like to reserve a table for four this evening at 7:00.

R I'm really sorry, but we're **fully booked** at 7:00. However, it will be available after 8:00.

G No. That's too late for us.

R I'm sorry, sir.

G **Never mind.** Thanks anyway.

R I would like to have a chance to serve you later. Thank you for your calling, sir.

Notes

- fully booked (예약이 꽉 찬)
- I'm really sorry, but we're fully booked. 정말 죄송합니다만 예약이 꽉 찼습니다.
- Never mind (걱정마세요)

Dialogue 7

R : Receptionist G : Guest

R Restaurant. How can I help you?

G Can you make a reservation for a table near the window for two? The name is Gilbert and we'd like to have lunch at 1:00.

R A table near the window for two at 1:00 for Mr. Gilbert, thank you.

G Thank you. Have a pleasant day.

Dialogue 8

R : Receptionist G : Guest

R Hello. Four Seasons Restaurant. May I help you?

G Yes, I want to make a reservation for tomorrow night.

R Tomorrow night? **What time do you have in mind?**

G At 7:30 in the evening.

R We have a **smoking and non-smoking section.** Which section do you **prefer**?

G Non-smoking, please.

R How many people?

G There will be three of us.

Notes

♠ have in mind 염두에 두다 생각하다

♠ smoking section 흡연구역 / non-smoking section 금연구역

♠ prefer 선호하다

Dialogue 9

R : Receptionist G : Guest

G I'd like to make a reservation for dinner.

R When would you like your table?

G At 7 o'clock in the evening.

R **In what name shall I make a reservation?**

G The name is David.

R How many persons in your party?

G A group of 10 people. If there is any change, I'll call you up.

R Many thanks.

Notes

♠ In what name shall I make a reservation? 누구 이름으로 예약할까요?
= Under what name shall I make a reservation?

♠ call (you) up 전화를 걸다 (미국 구어체)

♠ many thanks 매우 감사하다

Grammar

▣ Shall I ~

Shall I bring you a drink? Shall I show you to your seat now?

보기에서처럼 문장들을 매우 예의바른 표현의 허가를 나타내는 'Shall I~? 구문으로 고치시오.

1. The waiter wants to bring the appetizers first.
➡ Shall I bring your appetizers first?

2. The bartender wants to make the guest a cocktail.
➡ ______________________________ ?

3. The waitress will take the guest's orders.
➡ ______________________________ ?

4. The waiter will bring the guests their bill.

➡ ____ ?

5. The guest wants to pay the check right now.

➡ ____ ?

Restaurant English Tips

▣ 영어로 날짜 말하기

What date is it today? 오늘은 며칠입니까?

date는 날짜를 물어보는 질문이므로 요일을 묻는 질문인 What day is it today? 와 잘 구분해서 사용해야 한다.

1) 대답하는 법 : It's + 달 + 날, 연도
It's + 날 + of 달, 연도

예 : It's July twenty-first 2016. (2016년 7월 21일입니다)
It's (the) second of March 2016. (2016년 3월 2일입니다)

2) 날짜는 반드시 서수로 말함. 서수 앞에 the는 생략해도 좋다. '-th'의 발음에 유의

1일	first	11일	eleventh	21일	twenty-first
2일	second	12일	twelfth	22일	twenty-second
3일	third	13일	thirteenth	23일	twenty-third
4일	fourth	14일	fourteenth	24일	twenty-fourth
5일	fifth	15일	fifteenth	25일	twenty-fifth
6일	sixth	16일	sixteenth	26일	twenty-sixth
7일	seventh	17일	seventeenth	27일	twenty-seventh
8일	eighth	18일	eighteenth	28일	twenty-eighth

9일	ninth	19일	nineteenth	29일	twenty-ninth
10일	tenth	20일	twentieth	30일	thirtieth
				31일	thirty-first

특히 주의하여야 할 날짜와 서수 표현

1일	1st	4일	4th	12일	12th	22일	22nd	30일	30th
2일	2nd	10일	10th	20일	20th	23일	23rd	31일	31st
3일	3rd	11일	11th	21일	21st	24일	24th		

3) 연도 읽는 법

1999 두 자리씩 끊어서 읽는다. nineteen ninety nine

2015 천 자리에 끊어서 읽는다. two thousand fifteen

4) 영어로 화폐 단위 읽는 방법

영어에서는 뒤에서부터 세 자리씩 천 단위로 끊어서 읽는다.

천 단위마다 이름이 따로 있다.

▣ 1,000,000,000,000 won

trillion (조)	billion (10억)	million (100만)	thousand (천)

845,000 eight hundred (and) forty-five thousand

5,450,000 five million four hundred (and) fifty thousand

1,234,567,890 one billion two hundred (and) thirty-four million five hundred (and) sixty-seven thousand eight hundred (and) ninety

Review & Exercises

1. Words to memorize in this unit

reserve 예약하다
make a reservation 예약하다
fully booked 예약 완료된
party 일행(a party of two 일행 2명)
hold on 끊지 않고 기다리다
available 이용 가능한
non-smoking section 비흡연석
prefer 선호하다

2. Key expressions to memorize in this unit

1. What time are you open for lunch?
2. I'd like to reserve a table for tomorrow evening.
3. There is one table left by the window.
4. May I have your name and phone number please?
5. I'm really sorry, but we're fully booked.
6. Is there anything else I can do for you?
7. How many persons in your party?
8. In what name shall I make a reservation?
9. What time do you have in mind?
10. What can I do for you?

3. Exercises

1) Fill in the blank with the right prepositions

a. What time are you open ______ lunch?

b. Hold ______ please

c. There is one table left ______ the window

d. Is it ______ today?

e. A table ______ three ______ 8:00 tonight ______ Mr. Johnson.

f. ______ what time, sir?

g. Thank you ______ calling us.

2) Fill in the blank to complete the dialogue

R : Barney Restaurant. What ____________________?
(무엇을 도와드릴까요?)

G : Yes, I'd like to ________________ for four this evening at 7:00.
(오늘 저녁 7시에 4인 예약을 하려고 합니다)

R : I'm sorry, we're ____________________ at 7:00. However, it ________________ after 8:00.
(죄송하지만 7시에는 예약이 완료되었습니다. 하지만 8시 이후에는 이용 가능할 것입니다)

G : No. That's too late for us.

R : I'm sorry, sir.

G : Never _________. Thanks ___________.
(신경쓰지 마세요. 아무튼 감사합니다)

R : I would like to have a ____________________ you later. Thank you ________________, sir.
(나중에 당신에게 서비스할 수 있는 기회가 있으면 좋겠습니다.)

Restaurant Quiz

1. Lemons are generally (sweet, sour, bitter).
2. A menu is also sometimes known as a (postcard, bill of fare, check).
3. A rare steak is one which has been (cooked very little, cooked well enough, well seasoned).

Changing, Confirming & Cancelling the Reservation

Unit 2

Changing, Confirming & Cancelling the Reservation

Unit 2

Changing, Confirming & Cancelling the Reservation

Preview : Reading

▣ Order Taking

The key to your success as a waiter or waitress is salesmanship at the moment you take the order. You have the responsibility every time you take an order to help your guests select foods and beverages.

1. Know your menu first

You should make it a daily habit to check the special of the menu, and to note any changes in the items listed. Please find out what the ingredients of different dishes are and how long they take to prepare. This can be very important when a guest asks for suggestions.

2. Help your guest through suggestive selling

Try to analyze the average guest and find out what influences their choice of items. Is the menu going to help them? It's just confusing. You can turn their appetite on or off by the power of suggestion.

3. Make your suggestion colorful but specific.

Name only two items to give your guest an easy choice. It's easier to decide between two items than to pick from five or six.

4. The art of suggestion can work for you throughout the meal.

Remember that your guests are people. They expect your help with their food selections. Make your suggestions colorful and limit them to two items at a time to make it a pleasant meal.

▣ Key Words

salesmanship	판매정신	responsibility	책임감
daily	매일의	average	평균적인
note	주목하다	influence	영향을 주다
ingredient	식재료	confusing	혼동을 주는
suggestion	제안	appetite	입맛
through	-을 통해서	specific	구체적인
analyze	분석하다	selection	선택
throughout	-을 통털어서, 내내	suggestive	제안적인

▣ Reading Helper

웨이터로서 성공의 비결? 주문받는 순간 판매기법을 발휘하라.

고객의 식음료 품목 선택에 도와줄 책임이 있다.

1. 메뉴지식 숙지가 필요, 매일 당일의 특별 메뉴 및 메뉴 품목의 변동사항 확인을 습관화해야한다. 메뉴 품목별 식재료와 조리시간 숙지
2. 권유판매로 고객을 도와드려라. 식단은 혼동만 줄 뿐 당신의 권유 판매력이 고객의 식욕을 좌우한다.
3. 품목을 특정하여 다채롭게 설명하라. 고객이 쉽게 선택하도록 2개만 특정.

4. 권유판매 기법: 식사 과정 전체에 걸쳐 하면 효과적.
고객도 인간, 메뉴 선택에서 당신의 도움 기대할 때는 다채롭게, 2개 품목으로 한정, 즐거운 식사가 되게 하라.

Basic Vocabulary

▣ Fill in the blank with the meaning in Korean.

a bit		confirm	
cancel		expect	
serve		look forward to ~ing	
put off		commanding a good view	

Key Expressions

▣ Make a full sentence using the words given in the bracket.

1. 몇 시에 당신을 기대하면 될까요?
(What, expect, should, time, we, you, ?)

____

2. 전화 주셔서 감사합니다, 선생님.
(sir, you. for, thank, calling)

____

3. 내일 저녁은 어떠세요?

(about, evening, how, tomorrow, ?)

---

4 알려주셔서 감사합니다.

(know, letting, for, us, you, thank)

---

5. 다음에도 당신을 모실 수 있기를 바랍니다.

(hope, time, next, we, may, you, serve, we)

---

6. 오늘밤 테이블을 취소해야합니다.

(I, cancel, table, for, must, the, tonight)

---

7. 어느 분 성함으로 예약을 하셨습니까?

(a reservation, make, did, what, under, name, you, ?)

---

8. 혹시 당신의 예약을 변경시키거나 취소하실 거라면, 우리에게 알려주십시오.

(If, your, or, reservation, cancel, change, you / know, us, please, let)

---

9. 전망이 좋은 테이블로 예약해주세요.

(book, please, view, a table, commanding, good, a)

---

10. 내일 저녁 당신을 뵐 수 있기를 고대합니다.

(evening, you, to, look, we, forward, seeing, tomorrow)

Dialogues

Dialogue 1

R : Receptionist G : Guest

R Walker Hill Restaurant. May I help you?

G Yes, I'd like to reserve a table for three tomorrow.

R What time do you have in mind?

G At 2 p.m. Is it possible?

R Yes, we have a table by the window. May I have your name and phone number, please?

G My name is John and my phone number is 666-1234

R Well, is there anything else?

G No, that's alright. Thank you.

R You're welcome. **If you change or cancel your reservation, please let us know.** Thank you for your reservation.

Notes

- ♠ let us know 알려주세요.
- ♠ If you change or cancel your reservation, please let us know. 혹시 예약을 변경시키거나 취소하실 것이면 알려주십시오.

Dialogue 2

R : Receptionist G : Guest

G Sky Tower Restaurant? I've got **a group of 10 people.** We'd like to have dinner at your restaurant around 7.

R We're **a bit** busy at that time. **Could you make it** at 8?

G All right. We'll be there at 8. Please book for us a good table near the window **commanding a good view.**

R Yes, we will. **Thank you for calling.**

Notes

- ♠ a group of 10 people 10명 일행
  = 10 people in my party = a party of 10 people
- ♠ a bit = a little 약간
- ♠ Could you make it? 가능한가요?
- ♠ commanding a good view 전망이 좋은
- ♠ Thank you for calling. 전화 주셔서 감사합니다.

Dialogue 3

R : Receptionist G : Guest

R Sky Hill restaurant. May I help you?

G Yes. I'd like to make a reservation for a party of five for tonight at seven-thirty.

R We're **pretty busy** today. We have a table for eight o'clock but not at seven-thirty.

G That'll do.

R **Could I have your name,** please?

G Adams.

R All right Mr. Adams. Party of five for tonight at eight o'clock. Thank you for choosing our restaurant. Goodbye.

Notes

♠ pretty busy 제법 바쁘다

♠ Could I have your name? 성함이 어떻게 되십니까?

Dialogue 4

R : Receptionist G : Guest

R Evergreen Restaurant. Can I help you?

G Hello. I'd like to book a table for two for tonight.

R I'm sorry ma'am, but Saturday is our **busiest** night and we're fully booked this evening.

G I see. **How about** tomorrow evening, then?

R At what time?

G Eight o'clock.

R No problem. May I have your name, please?

G It's Jones. J–O–N–E–S.

R Thank you Ms. Jones. We **look forward to** seeing you tomorrow evening.

G Thank you. Goodbye.

Notes

♠ busiest 가장 바쁜 (busy의 최상급) (Grammar 설명 참조)

♠ How about ~? ~는 어떠세요?

♠ look forward to ~ing ~을 학수고대하다

Dialogue 5

R : Receptionist G : Guest

G Is this the Green Restaurant?

R Yes, ma'am. How may I help you?

G Yes. I'm really sorry. I made a reservation for a table for three for lunch tomorrow at 12:00, but I have to cancel my reservation.

R Who made the reservation?

G Mrs. Brown.

R **Thank you for letting us know. We hope we may serve you next time.**

G I hope so, too. Good bye.

Notes

♠ Thank you for letting us know. 알려주셔서 감사합니다.

♠ We hope we may serve you next time. 다음에도 모실 수 있기를 바랍니다.

Dialogue 6

R : Receptionist G : Guest

R Good morning, this is the Pearl Restaurant. May I help you?

G Yes, this is Park. I reserved a table for three at 7:00 tonight, but I must cancel the table for tonight and **put it off till tomorrow** at the same time.

R All right, Mr. Park. You'll have a table for three at 7:00 tomorrow evening.

G I'm sorry for the change. Thank you.

R Not at all, sir. We look forward to seeing you tomorrow. Good-bye.

Notes

♠ put it off till tomorrow 내일까지 미루다

Dialogue 7

R : Receptionist G : Guest

R Good afternoon! This is Green Palace. May I help you?

G Yes, I made a reservation tomorrow, a table for five, and I'd like to confirm it.

R **Under what name did you make a reservation?**

G It's Veronica.

R Yes, Ms. Veronica. **Your reservation is confirmed,** and it is on the list.

G Thanks.

R You're welcome. We'll be expecting you.

Notes

♠ Under what name did you make a reservation? 누구 이름으로 예약하셨습니까?

♠ Your reservation is confirmed 예약이 확인되었다. (수동태에 유의)

Grammar

1. 형용사 비교급과 최상급 만들기

1) 1음절 형용사는 ~er ~est를 붙인다.

예) clean – cleaner – cleanest cheap – cheaper – cheapest

2) 2음절 중에서 y로 끝나는 형용사는 ~ier ~iest를 붙인다.

예) dirty – dirtier – dirtiest easy – easier – easiest

3) 긴 단어들은 대체로 more, most를 붙인다.

예) polite – more polite – the most polite

beautiful, interesting, comfortable, courageous

4) 불규칙 형용사는 암기하여야 한다.

good / well – better – the best

bad / ill – worse – the worst

much/many – more – the most

little – less – the least

old – elder(older) – the eldest(oldest)

5) 다음 형용사들의 비교급과 최상급을 써보라.

bright		easy	
good		wonderful	
hot		friendly	
cold		bad	
healthy		intelligent	
tall		sunny	
heavy		honest	
large		early	

2. 비교문 연습

1) 비교하는 문장에서는 -er than, 혹은 more - than, not as - as 등의 구문을 사용한다.

> The Italian wine is sweeter than the New Zealand wine.
> The French wine is more expensive than the Chilean.
> The New Zealand wine isn't as dry as the Portuguese.

2) 다음 공란을 비교급으로 채워 문장을 완성하시오.

a. The restaurant is ____________ (busy) tonight than last weekend.

b, The Plaza is ____________ (close) to the airport than the Grand.

c. A suite is ____________ (expensive) than a single room.

d. I think the Sauvignon Blanc is ____________ (good) than the Riesling.

e. Mineral water is ____________ (cheap) than wine.

f. The Chilean Merlot is ________________ (not smooth) as the French Merlot.

Restaurant English Tips

1. 시각 읽는 법

7:00 At seven o'clock, At seven

7:15 At seven fifteen, At a quarter past seven

7:30 At seven thirty, At half past seven

7:45 At seven forty-five, At a quarter to eight

2. 날짜 읽는 법

2017년 1월 1일

적을 때 : 1 Jan. 2017

말할 때 : On January first, two thousand seventeen

(OR) The first of January, two thousand seventeen

3. 연습문제

다음 날짜와 시각을 영어 혹은 숫자로 나타내시오.

1. Nine oh five ________________
2. Quarter to four ________________
3. Four thirty ________________
4. Quarter past eleven ________________
5. Quarter to eight ________________
6. Half past two ________________
7. February twelfth, two thousand sixteen ________________
8. 2017년 3월 20일 ________________
9. 1998년 10월 12일 ________________
10. (Your Birthday) ________________

Review & Exercises

1. Words to memorize in this unit

a bit 약간
pretty 제법
cancel 취소하다
serve 서비스하다
put off 연기하다
confirm 확인하다
expect 기대하다
look forward to ~ing ~을 기대하다
commanding a good view 전망 좋은

2. Key expressions to memorize in this unit

1. What time should we expect you?
2. Thank you for calling, sir.
3. How about tomorrow evening?
4. Thank you for letting us know.
5. We hope we may serve you next time.
6. I must cancel the table for tonight.
7. Under what name did you make a reservation?
8. If you change or cancel your reservation, please let us know.
9. Please book a table commanding a good view.
10. We look forward to seeing you tomorrow evening.

3. Exercise

1) Fill in the blank with the suitable preposition.

a. How _______ tomorrow evening?

b. We look forward _______ seeing you tomorrow evening.

c. I must cancel the table for tonight and put it _______ till tomorrow.

d. _______ what name did you make a reservation?

2) Fill in the blank to complete the dialogue

R : Evergreen Restaurant. Can I help you?

G : Hello. I'd like ____________________ for two for tonight.

(오늘밤 2인 테이블을 예약하고 싶습니다)

R : I'm sorry ma'am, but Saturday is our busiest night and we're ____________________ this evening.

(오늘 저녁에는 예약이 만료되었습니다)

G : I see. ______________ tomorrow evening, then?

(내일 저녁은 어떠세요?)

R : At what time?

G : Eight o'clock.

R : No problem. ____________________, please?

(성함이 어떻게 되십니까?)

G : it's Jones. J-O-N-E-S.

R : Thank you Ms. Jones. We look ____________________ tomorrow evening.

(뵙기를 고대하고 있겠습니다)

Restaurant Quiz

1. To whip is to (enjoy, beat, drink).
2. The yellow part of an egg is known as the (shell, yolk, white).
3. The covering or skin of any fruit is generally referred to as the (heart, top, peel).

Welcoming & Seating the Guest

Unit 3

Welcoming & Seating the Guest

Unit 3

Welcoming & Seating the Guest

레스토랑은 호텔 Dining Room 중에서 격식 및 격조 있는 식당으로서, 메뉴 가격이 높은 편이며 정교한 서비스가 특징이다. 종사원은 대부분 숙련된 Staff으로 구성되어 있고, 때로는 고객에게도 Dress Code를 원하기도 한다.

Preview : Reading

▣ Welcoming & Seating the Guest

When entering a restaurant there is usually a greeter (sometimes called a host or hostess) who leads people to their seats and gives them their menus. In some cases, it is necessary for the guests to make reservations in advance. Generally the following sequence will cover most situations:

1) Promptly acknowledge the guests and welcome them with a greeting. An example of this may be: "Good evening, welcome to Grand Hotel."

2) Ask if the customer has a reservation. If customers don't have a reservation, the service staff must make sure that there is a table

available. If the guests have a reservation, service staff should check the number of expected guests for the table.

3) Show guests to their table.

4) At the table, pull out one chair for the guests.

▣ Key Words

greeter	맞이하는 사람	acknowledge	인정하다
in advance	미리	customer	고객
generally	일반적으로	make sure	확인하다
sequence	연쇄, 연속	available	이용가능한
situation	상황	expected	기대되는
promptly	즉각적으로	pull out	잡아 빼다

▣ Reading Helper

식당 입장 시 맞이해주고 메뉴를 주는 사람이 있다. 대략 이 순서대로 진행.

1. 손님임을 즉각적으로 인지하고 인사로 맞이함
2. 예약여부 확인. 무예약시 가능한 테이블 있는지 확인, 예약시 기대한 손님의 숫자 확인
3. 테이블로 안내
4. 일행 중 한명의 의자를 당겨줌. 자리가 확보되었다는 의미

▣ Review of the Reading

1. 미리 예약하다 make a reservation in ____________

2. 다음 일련의 행동이 대부분 상황에 해당될 것이다. the following s______________ will cover most situations.

3. 손님임을 즉각적으로 알아차려라 P__________ acknowledge the guests

4. 이용 가능한 테이블 table a__________

5. 기대되어지는 손님의 수 the number of e__________ guests

Basic Vocabulary

■ Fill in the blank with the meaning in Korean.

booth	view
by any chance	rib
take order	baked
crowded	medium rare
aisle	sour
seat	by the way
command	shortly
colleague	

Key Expressions

■ Make a full sentence using the words given in the bracket.

1. 이쪽으로 오세요.
(please, way, come, this)

____

2. 20분 정도 기다리셔도 되겠습니까?
(minutes, for, mind, would, 20, waiting, you, ?)

3. 주문 받으러 다시 오겠습니다.
(be, to, your, I'll, back, take, order)

4. 통로 쪽에 테이블이 하나 있습니다.
(There, aisle, is, by, a table, the)

5. 스테이크를 어떻게 구워 드릴까요?
(steak, like, would, how, your, you, ?)

6. 그것은 한강의 아름다운 전망이 있습니다.
(It, Han River, a, commands, the, view, beautiful, of)

7. 이 테이블 마음에 드세요?
(How, you, table, like, do, this, ?)

8. 곧 다시 오겠습니다 선생님.
(I'll, a moment, in, right, be, back, sir)

____

9. 라운지에 앉아 계시지요?
(don't, a seat, lounge, in, have, the, why, you, ?)

____

10. 지금 2인용 테이블이 있습니까?
(you, do, a table, now, two, for, have, ?)

____

Dialogues

Dialogue 1

R : Receptionist G : Guest

R Do you have a reservation, sir?

G Yes, I'm Jay Park. I reserved a table for two.

R Yes, Mr. Park. A party of two. **Come this way.** Is this table all right?

G I don't like a booth. Do you **by any chance** have a table near the window?

R **I'm afraid** we don't.

Notes

♠ Come this way. 이쪽으로 오십시오
= Step this way.
= Follow me
= Come with me
♠ by any chance 혹시
♠ I'm afraid ~ ~일 것 같다 (완곡어법)
I'm afraid it will rain soon. 비가 곧 올 것 같다.

Dialogue 2

R : Receptionist G : Guest

R Good evening, sir. Do you have a reservation?

G No, I thought there might be a table available.

R I'm sorry, but we are fully booked tonight. Would you mind waiting for 20 minutes? A table will be available by then.

G Oh, really? I will wait.

R If you like, you can have a drink in the lounge. May I have your name?

G Davis, Thomas Davis.

R How many members are in your party?

G Five all together.

R I'll let you know when the table is ready.

G Thank you.

Notes

♠ 고객에게 인사할 때는 Good morning, Good afternoon 등으로 인사한다. 'Hello'라는 말은 쓰지 않고, 인사말 후에는 반드시 'sir'나 'madam/ma'am'을 붙인다.

♠ Would you mind ~ing? ~하셔도 괜찮으시겠습니까?
대답은 "Not at all"로 답을 해야 괜찮다는 의미가 되므로 주의할 것.

♠ May I have your name? 성함이 어떻게 되십니까?

♠ all together 모두 합해서

♠ I'll let you know ~ 제가 알려 드리겠습니다.

Dialogue 3

R : Receptionist G : Guest

R How many in your party?

G Just two.

R Did you make a reservation?

G No, I didn't.

R But no problem. Step this way, please.

G This is a nice seat. Thanks.

R **I'll be back to take your order.**

Notes

♠ I'll be back to take your order. 주문 받으러 다시 오겠습니다

Dialogue 4

R : Receptionist G : Guest

R Good evening, sir

G A table for two, please.

R Do you have a reservation?

G No we don't. Is it possible to have dinner?

R Certainly. Smoking or non-smoking?

G Non-smoking, please.

R Could you follow me, please? Just here, sir.

G What about that one?

R I'm sorry, that table is already reserved.

Dialogue 5

R : Receptionist G : Guest

G It looks **a bit crowded.**

R There is **a table by the aisle.**

G Do you have a table by the window?

R I'm sorry but the table by the aisle is the only one.

G OK I'll take it.

R Come this way, please. **Please take a seat.** Will this be fine?

G Thanks.

R **My colleague, Sarah will be with you shortly.** Enjoy your breakfast.

Notes

♠ a bit crowded 약간 붐빈다

= a bit busy
= a bit packed

♠ a table by the aisle. 통로 옆 테이블
c.f. a table by the window 창가 쪽 테이블
aisle seat / window seat / middle seat / center seat

♠ aisle /ail/ 통로 (발음에 유의)

♠ Please take a seat. 앉으세요.

♠ My colleague, Sarah will be with you shortly. 제 동료인 Sarah가 곧 올 것입니다.

♠ shortly 곧, 오래지 않아

Dialogue 6

R : Receptionist G : Guest

R Good evening. May I know how many are in your party?

G Two.

R Please come this way. I'll seat you by the window.

G Thank you. It commands a beautiful view of the Han River. Let me have a menu.

R Here it is. Would you like something from the bar before you order your main dish?

G Martini.

(A little later)

R Excuse me, this is our bread and a dip with a compli-mentary welcome appetizer. Enjoy it. Are you ready to order now, sir?

G I'll have the prime rib with a baked potato.

R How would you like your steak?

G Medium rare.

R Good. Do you want butter and sour cream on your potato?

G Yes. Thanks a lot.

Notes

- May I know how many are in your party? 일행이 몇 분인지 여쭤봐도 될까요?
- I'll seat you 자리를 정해 드리겠습니다
- It commands a beautiful view of the Han River. 한강의 아름다운 전망이 있다
- dip = dip sauce 빵을 적셔 먹는 소스
- a complimentary welcome appetizer 환영의 뜻으로 무료로 드리는 애피타이즈
- How would you like your steak? 스테이크를 어떻게 요리해 드릴까요?
- medium rare 중간보다 덜 익힌
  well done 완전히 익힌
  rare 거의 익히지 않은

Dialogue 7

R : Receptionist G : Guest

R How are you this evening, sir?

G I'm just great, and you?

R Fine, sir. Did you make a reservation?

G Yes, a table for two at 7:30.

R Would you come this way, please? How do you like this table?

G That would be great.

R These are our menus. I'll be right back in a moment, sir.

Notes

- ♠ How do you like this table? 이 테이블이 마음에 드십니까?
- ♠ I'll be right back in a moment. 잠시 후 바로 다시 오겠습니다

Dialogue 8

R : Receptionist G : Guest(Walk-in Guest)

R Good evening. May I help you?

G Hello. Do you have a table for two now?

R By the way, sir, do you have a reservation?

G No, we just arrived here.

R I'm sorry, the restaurant is full at this moment, but we will make a table for you in about half an hour. Would it be possible to wait for a while, sir?

G O.K.

R Why don't you have a seat in the lounge, and we will let you know when the table is ready.

G All right, my name's Smith.

Notes

- ♠ Walk-in guest 예약 없이 걸어 들어온 손님.
- ♠ Do you have a table for two now? 지금 2인 테이블이 있습니까?
- ♠ By the way 그런데
- ♠ Why don't you ~ ? ~하지 그래요.
- ♠ let you know 알려 드리겠습니다

Grammar

1. a/an, the

처음 대화할 때에는 a/an 사용. 두번째로 언급할 때, 또 그것이 무엇인지 분명할 때는 the를 사용한다.

> We have **a** reservation. **The** reservation is for eight o'clock.
> I'd like **an** aperitif, please.
> Is this **the** menu?

다음 공란을 채우시오.

1) Can we have ______ adjoining room?
2) What's ______ dish of the day?
3) Could we have ______ table for four?
4) Put _____ olive on a cocktail stick. Then, put _____ olive in the glass.
5) Yes, the hotel has ______ car park.
6) Put some crushed ice into ______ cocktail shaker.

2. a/an, some

a/an은 one의 대신이다. some은 헤아릴 수 없는 명사에 쓰인다.

> I'd like **a** bottle of wine. I'd like **an** aperitif.

셀 수 있는 명사(countable noun)는 단수 복수를 구분해야 한다. 셀 수 없는 명사에는 some, much를 쓴다.

I' d like **some** bread, **some** water and **some** milk.

셀 수 있는 명사	vegetable, egg, carrot, onion, mushroom 등
셀 수 없는 명사	water, wine, rice, fish, beef, chicken, pepper, salt, sugar, garlic, lettuce, spinach, mustard, sauce, sesame oil 등

다음 중 맞는 것을 고르시오.

1) I have (many/much) books.
2) I need ______ (an/some) oil and ______ (an/some) egg.
3) There are ______ (a/some) people in the room.
4) I saw _____ (a/many) hero from the war _____ (an/some) hour ago.
5) ______ (some/much) apples are here.
6) You can drink ______(a/some) water.
7) How ______ (much/many) money do you have?
8) He went to university in ______ (a/some) small town.

3. Practice

다음 공란을 a/an, some으로 채우시오.

1) Would you like ______ wine?
2) ______ bottle of Chablis, please.
3) Could we have ______ bread?
4) Would you like ______ aperitif?
5) Could I have ______ ice in my Coke?
6) Could you call me ______ taxi?
7) Just ______ glass of red wine, please.
8) I want to change ______ money.

Restaurant English Tips

▣ Steak and Eggs

1. Steak Temperature

Rare 2~3분

Medium-Rare 3~4분

Medium 5~6분

Medium-welldone 8~9분

Welldone 10~12분

2. 식사를 주문할 때 알아두어야 할 계란 요리

(1) fried egg 프라이 계란

1) sunny-side up 계란의 한쪽 면만 프라이한 요리

2) over easy 계란의 양쪽 면을 프라이하되 노른자는 익히지 않음

3) over medium 계란의 흰자를 완전히 프라이하고 노른자를 살짝 익힌 것

4) over hard 흰자와 노른자를 완전히 프라이한 계란

5) turned over 계란의 양쪽 면을 프라이한 요리

(2) scrambled egg 스크램블 계란

우유를 섞어 휘저은 계란을 팬에 휘저으며 요리한 계란. 우유 또는 생크림을 넣고 잘 휘저은 다음 가열된 프라이팬에 휘저은 계란을 넣고 빨리 저어야한다. 엔초비. 감자 .버섯, 새우, 치즈 등을 넣어 만들기도 한다

(3) boiled egg 삶은 계란

물은 끓는 온도보다 조금 낮은 93℃ 정도의 물에 계란의 껍질을 깨지 않고 삶은 계란요리

1) soft boiled egg(미숙) 3~4분

2) medium boiled egg (반숙) 5~6분

3) hard boiled egg (완숙) 10~12분

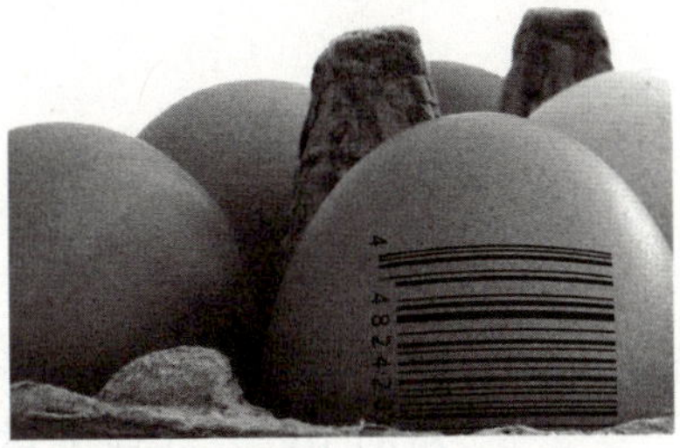

(4) poached egg 수란

계란을 소량의 소금과 식초를 넣어 약하게 끓는 물에 계란 껍질을 제거하고 삶은 요리로서 soft, medium, hard 등을 주문할 수 있다.

1) soft poached egg 3~4분정도

2) medium poached egg 5~6분정도

3) hard poached egg 8~9분정도

(5) omlet 계란 말이

ham, cheese, 양송이, 양파, 피망 등을 곁들여서 계란을 요리한다. 보기 좋은 크기와 형태를 만들기 위해 보통 계란 3개를 사용하여 만든다. 다른 재료를 섞지 않고 계란만 말아서 만든 것을 plain omelet 이라고 하고 ham bacon, cheese, mushroom 등을 속에 넣어서 만들기도 한다

3. 고기류

(1) veal 송아지고기 (2) calf 어린 송아지고기

(3) pork 돼지고기 (4) lamb 양고기

(5) chicken 닭고기 (6) turkey 칠면조

Review & Exercises

1. Words to memorize in this unit

booth 부스, 칸막이 좌석 take order 주문 받다

by any chance 혹시 crowded 붐비는

aisle 통로 복도

seat 자리에 앉히다

colleague 동료

shortly 곧, 오래지 않아

command (경치를) 향하다

view 전망

rib 갈비

baked 구운

medium rare 중간보다 덜 익힌

sour 신맛의

by the way 그런데

2. Key expressions to memorize in this unit

1. Come this way, please
2. Would you mind waiting for 20 minutes?
3. I'll be back to take your order.
4. There is a table by the aisle.
5. How would you like your steak?
6. It commands a beautiful view of the Han River.
7. How do you like this table?
8. I'll be right back in a moment, sir.
9. Why don't you have a seat in the lounge?
10. Do you have a table for two now?

3. Exercises

1) Fill in the blank with the suitable preposition.

a. Do you ______ any chance have a table near the window?

b. Do you have a table ______ the window?

c. I'll be right back ______ a moment, sir.

d. I'm sorry, the reservation is full ______ this moment

e. We will make a table for you ______ about half an hour.

2) Pair Activities

우리말 뜻에 맞게 공란을 채우고 파트너와 연습하세요.

(1)

R : How are you this evening, sir?

G : I'm just great, and you?

R : Fine, sir. Did you ________________?

(예약은 하셨나요?)

G : Yes, a table for two at 7:30

R : Would you ____________________, please.

(이쪽으로 와 주시겠어요?)

How do you like ____________________?

(이 테이블이 마음에 드세요?)

G : That would be great.

R : I'll be ______________________ a moment, sir.

(곧 다시 돌아오겠습니다)

(2)

R : Good evening. May I help you?

G : Hello. Do you have a table for two now?

R : By the way, sir, do you ________________?

(예약은 하셨나요?)

G : No, we just arrived in here.

R : I'm sorry, the restaurant is full ________________, but we can make a ________________________ in about half an hour. Would it be possible to ________________, sir?

(지금은 꽉 찼습니다만 30분 후면 자리를 마련해 드리겠습니다. 잠시만 기다리는 것이 가능하시겠습니까?)

G : O.K

R : Why don't you ____________________ in the lounge, and we will let you know when ________________________________.

(라운지에 앉아 계시겠어요? 테이블이 준비되면 알려드리겠습니다.)

G : All right, my name's Smith.

Restaurant Quiz

1. To be allergic to something is to be (fond of it, sensitive to it, crazy about it).
2. Extra means (a few, some, additional).
3. Hamburger is normally made from (chopped beef, liver, roast pork).

Chapter 2

Order Taking & Meal Services

여행에서 식사는 각 나라의 토속적인 맛을 볼 수 있는 즐거움이다. 호텔의 아침식사는 주로 buffet style이 많으나 별도의 주문을 받는 경우도 있다. 레스토랑에서는 식당 입구에 'Please wait to be seated'(앉을 자리로 안내할 때까지 기다려 주시오)라는 팻말이 있는 경우에는 waiter가 와서 안내해 줄 때까지 기다린다. 식사 주문 시에는 starter 혹은 appetizer(식욕을 돋우는 음식이나 술), main dish(본 음식), salad(샐러드), dessert(후식) 등에 대해 취향대로 주문하며 식사예절에 벗어나지 않도록 주의한다.

나는 레스토랑 영어다

Breakfast

Unit 4

Breakfast

Unit **4**

Breakfast

Preview : Reading

▣ Hotel Breakfast

The types of hotel breakfasts are the Continental breakfast, American breakfast, Japanese breakfast, Korean breakfast etc. There are also a wide variety of á la carte dishes: juices, pancakes, toast or eggs.

The American breakfast, popular with businessmen, is not confined to Americans. Generally speaking, the American breakfast consists of fruit juice, potato and two eggs, some bacon, ham or sausage, and coffee or tea.

The Continental breakfast is also popular with business people. It is a light but sufficient breakfast. The Continental breakfast does not include potatoes and eggs as in the American breakfast. It is typically eaten in European countries, especially France and Italy, and it consists of croissants or bread rolls, butter, jam, and coffee.

▣ Key Words

a variety of	다양한	consist of ~	~로 구성되다
á la carte	정식메뉴	sufficient	충분한
confine	한정하다	typically	전형적으로

▣ Reading Helper

1. American breakfast 미국식 조찬(달걀 요리를 중심으로 하여 주스 혹은 과일, 씨리얼, 빵, 소시지, 커피로 구성되는 아침 식사)
2. Continental breakfast 대륙식 조찬(달걀 요리가 없이 커피, 빵, 주스 정도의 간단한 아침식사)

▣ Review of the Reading

1. The ____________ breakfast consists of fruit juice, potato and two eggs, some bacon, ham or sausage, and coffee or tea.

2. The ____________ breakfast consists of croissants or bread rolls, butter, jam, and coffee.

Basic Vocabulary

▣ Fill in the blank with the meaning in Korean.

slice		peach	
mashed		stewed	
heavy / light		wedge	
prune		assorted	
crisp		season	

dark or light	watermelon
raisin	

Key Expressions

▣ **Make a full sentence using the words given in the bracket.**

1. 아침 식사로 무엇을 드시겠습니까?
   (would, breakfast, like, you, what, for, ?)

   ____

2. 계란을 어떻게 해 드릴까요?
   (eggs, how, you, like, your, would, ?)

   ____

3. 주문하실 준비가 되셨나요?
   (order, ready, are, to, you, ?)

   ____

4. 마실 것 좀 드시겠어요?
   (would, drink, to, like, you, anything, ?)

   ____

5. 오늘의 특별 메뉴가 무엇이지요?
   (menu, what, today's, is, special, ?)

   ____

6. 무엇을 마시겠습니까 부인?
(What, like, you, would, drink, to, ma'am, ?)

7. 어떤 종류의 음료수가 있습니까?
(have, do, of, what, you, drinks, kind, ?)

8. 주문 받아도 되겠습니까?
(order, take, may, your, I, ?)

9. 저에게는 미국식 조찬을 주세요.
(Let, breakfast, the, American, have, me)

10. 그것들은 현재 제 철이 아닙니다.
(season, are, now, not, in, they)

Dialogues

Dialogue 1

W : Waiter G : Guest

W Good morning, sir! What would you like for breakfast?

G Two eggs and ham.

W How would you like your eggs?

G Sunny-side up, please.

W How about coffee?

G No, thanks.

Notes

♠ what would you like for breakfast?
for dessert
for drink

♠ how would you like your eggs?
coffee
steak

♠ How about having coffee? (커피는 어떠세요?)
What about having coffee?
Why don't you have coffee?

Dialogue 2

W : Waiter G : Guest

W Good morning. **Are you ready to order?**

G Yes, I am, thank you. I'll have three scrambled eggs with country ham, toast and jam, please.

W **Would you like anything to drink?**

G I'll have a tomato juice and some iced tea.

W Anything else?

G Could I have **a slice of** pumpkin pie?

W Sure. **Coming right up.**

Notes

♠ Are you ready to order? 주문하시겠어요?

♠ Would you like anything to drink? 마실 것 좀 드시겠어요?

♠ a slice of = a piece of 한 조각의

♠ Coming right up: 곧바로 준비해드리겠습니다

Dialogue 3

W : Waiter G : Guest

W Good morning. May I help you?

G Yes, we'd like to order breakfast.

W What would you like?

G I'd like some carrot juice, two eggs sunny-side up with two sausages, **hash-browns** and tea.

W Thank you. And for you, ma'am?

G I'll have grapefruit juice, two scrambled eggs with bacon, toast and coffee, please.

W Certainly

Notes

♠ hash-brown 해쉬브라운, 잘게 쪼갠 감자를 넓적하게 구운 요리

Dialogue 4

W : Waiter G : Guest

W Good morning, ma'am. What would you like for breakfast?

G **What is today's special menu?**

W It's special steak.

G Oh It's too **heavy.** I want something **light.**

W Then would you like **mashed** potatoes and some bread?

G Sounds good. I'll take it.

W What would you like to drink, ma'am?

G **What kind of drinks do you have?**

W Orange juice, coke, coffee and green tea.

G Green tea, please.

W Anything else?

G Ice green tea, please.

W Very well, ma'am. I'll bring it right away.

Notes

♠ What is today's special menu? 오늘의 특별 메뉴가 무엇이지요?

♠ heavy : (위에) 부담되는

♠ mashed : 으깬

♠ light : (소화하기) 쉬운, 가벼운

♠ What kind of drinks do you have?

dessert

Dialogue 5

W : Waiter G : Guest

W **Have you decided on what you would like?**

G I want to have the American breakfast.

W How would you like your eggs?

G Turned over, please.

W I see. What would you like to drink?

G Please bring me a glass of orange juice.

W OK. What kind of dessert would you like?

G Ice cream, please

W Thank you. Coming right up.

(After meal)

W Did you enjoy your meal, ma'am?

G Yes it was great. Can I have the bill?

W Oh, it is in the stand on your table.

G I see. Thank you.

W We hope to serve you again.

Notes

♠ Have you decided on what you would like? 드시고 싶은 것을 결정하셨나요?

= Would you like to order?

= May I take your order?

Dialogue 6

W : Waitress **G** : Guest

W Good morning, sir. What would you like for breakfast?

G Two eggs and ham.

W How would you like your eggs?

G Sunny-side up.

W How about coffee?

G No, thanks.

Dialogue 7

W : Waiter **G** : Guest

W Good morning. **May I take your order?**

G Yes, please. I'd like a **Continental breakfast.**

W Yes, ma'am. **You have a choice of orange, tomato, or grapefruit juice.**

G OK. Tomato, please.

W Coffee or tea?

G Coffee with cream, please.

Notes

♠ Continental breakfast : 대륙식 조찬. 달걀 요리가 없이 커피, 빵, 주스 정도의 간단한 식사. 객실 요금에 아침 식사 요금이 포함됨. American breakfast에서 쏘세지와 계란 요리가 빠짐.

♠ You have a choice of orange, tomato, or grapefruit juice.
bacon or sausage
strawberry vanilla or chocolate ice cream

Dialogue 8

W : Waiter G : Guest

W Ready to order now?

G Let me have the American breakfast.

W How would you like your eggs?

G Over-easy with bacon.

W I see, and what would you like to drink?

G Tea with a wedge of lemon.

Notes

♠ a wedge of 한 조각의

Dialogue 9

W : Waitress G : Guest

W Good morning, sir. May I take your order, please?

G1 I'm not so hungry now. I'd like to have just a Continental breakfast.

W Would you like to have orange juice or tomato juice?

G1 Fresh tomato juice, please.

W Would you like anything, sir?

G2 Coffee, please. I'd like to have an American breakfast. Do you have pineapple?

W Of course, sir.

G2 Pineapple, fried eggs, ham, dark toast and a cup of hot milk, please.

W Yes, sir. Thank you.

Dialogue 10

W : Waiter G : Guest

W Good morning. Here's the menu, sir. Are you ready to order now?

G I'd like to have a choice of **assorted fresh fruits in season.** What kind of fruits are there now?

W Pineapples, bananas, strawberries and papayas are in season now.

G Bring the fruits, except papayas. Don't you have any fresh watermelons and peaches?

W I'm sorry. **They are not in season now.** We have **stewed prunes** and apple sauce.

G No, I prefer fresh fruits, bacon crisp and two **poached eggs.**

W Would you like anything to drink?

G Orange juice, please.

Notes

♠ assorted fresh fruits : 여러 가지 신선한 과일을 골고루 차린

♠ in season : 제 철의 (c.f. out of season)

♠ They are not in season now. 그것들은 제 철이 아닙니다

♠ stewed prune 뭉근하게 죽같이 끓인 자두

♠ poached egg : 수란

Dialogue 11

W : Waitress G : Guest

W May I take your order now, sir?

G Yes, I'm very hungry. Bring me an **English breakfast** as soon as possible.

W Yes, sir. How would you like your steak? **Dark or light?**

G Medium. Bring me corn flakes with raisins and sausage.

W How would you like your eggs?

G Over-hard, please.

W What would you like to drink, sir?

G Please bring me a glass of orange juice.

W Yes, sir. I'll bring them right away.

(Fifteen minutes later)

W Would you like anything else, sir? Would you like some more orange juice?

G A little more orange juice, please.

W Thank you, sir.

Notes

♠ English breakfast : American breakfast에 생선요리가 추가됨.

♠ dark or light : 바싹 구울까요 덜 구울까요? (스테이크의 굽는 정도)

Grammar

1. I'll have ~

I'll have the shrimp cocktail.

I think **I'll have** the filet mignon.

위 보기에서처럼 주문 할 때에 "I'll have"라는 표현을 쓴다.

다음 문장들을 "I'll have~"를 사용해서 주문을 해 보시오.

1) Let me have a salad with ranch dressing.

➡ ____.

2) I'll take the beef lasagna, please.

➡ ____.

3) Let me have another glass of wine.

➡ ____.

4) I'll take the seafood platter, please.

➡ ____.

5) Let me have a Vodka Martini.

➡ ____.

6) I'll take a slice of cherry pie of dessert, please.

➡ ____.

2. Is it possible to ~?

"Is it possible to ~?"를 사용하여 가능한지를 정중하게 물을 수 있다. 보기처럼 의문문을 만들어 보시오.

> **Is it possible to** order room service here?
> **Is it possible to** get some food delivered to my room?

1) You want to change your order.

➡ Is it possible to change my order?

2) You want to order something unusual.

➡ ____?

3) You'd like to cancel your reservation.

➡ ____?

4) You'd like to stay an extra day.

➡ ____?

5) You'd like to connect to the Internet.

➡ ____?

Restaurant English Tips

▣ Breakfast의 종류

1. American Breakfast(미국식 조찬)

달걀 요리를 중심으로 주스 혹은 과일, 씨리얼, 빵, 계란, 소시지, 커피로 구성되는 아침 식사. 신선한 주스, 빵, 계란요리 그리고 커피나 홍차로 구성되어 제공한다. 계란요리에는 ham, bacon, sausage중에서 한가지와 감자튀김이 곁들어진다. 여기에 sole(서대기) 또는 halibut(넙치) 같은 생선구이가 추가되면 영국식 아침식사(English breakfast)가 된다.

구성 내용

A choice of juices
Breakfast of roll & toast
Two eggs any style
Ham, bacon or sausage
Coffee or tea

2. Continental breakfast(대륙식 조찬)

영국식 아침식사와 구별하기 위하여 대륙식 조식이라고 하며 주스 빵 커피나 홍차로 구성되어 제공되는 간단한 아침식사이다. 달걀 요리가 없이 커피, 빵, 주스 정도의 간단한 식사이다. 객실 요금에 아침 식사 요금이 포함된다. American breakfast에서 소시지와 계란 요리가 빠진다.

구성 내용

A choice of juices
Breakfast of roll & toast
Coffee or tea

3. English breakfast(영국식 조찬)

American breakfast에 생선요리가 추가된다.

Review & Exercises

1. Words to memorize in this unit

slice 조각
mashed 으깬
heavy/light 식사량이 많은/ 가벼운
wedge 조각
assorted 종류별로 모은
season 계절, 양념
watermelon 수박
peach 복숭아
stewed 죽같이 끓인
prune 자두
crisp 바삭바삭한
dark or light 많이 구울까요 가볍게 구울까요?
raisin 건포도

2. Key expressions to memorize in this unit

1. What would you like for breakfast?
2. How would you like your eggs?

3. Are you ready to order?

4. Would you like anything to drink?

5. What is today's special menu?

6. What would you like to drink, ma'am?

7. What kind of drinks do you have?

8. May I take your order?

9. Let me have the American breakfast.

10. They are not in season now.

3. Exercises

1) Fill in the blank with the suitable preposition.

a. Have you decided ______ what you would like?

b. They are not ______ season now.

c. I'll bring them right ______.

d. Coming right ______.

2) Pair Activity (1)

우리말 뜻에 맞도록 공란을 채우고 파트너와 연습하세요.

W : Waitress G : Guest

W : Good morning, sir. ______________________________ breakfast?

(아침 식사로 무엇을 드시겠습니까?)

G : Two eggs and ham.

W : How ____?

(계란은 어떻게 요리해드릴까요?)

G : ________________________. (한 면만 후라이 해 주세요)

W : How about coffee?

G : ___________________________. (고맙지만 사양할게요)

2) Pair Activity (2)

Practice the conversation with your partner. Use the information in the box below.

A : Have you decided what you would like to order?

B : Yes. For starters, I'll have the ________________

A : Very good. And what would you like for an entrée?

B : Everything looks good. But I think I'll have the ______.

A : That's an excellent choice. Shall I bring you a drink?

B : Yes, I'd like to have __________.

A : I'll bring that to you immediately. Will there be anything else?

B : No, that will be it for now.

Appetizer	entrée	Drink
Caesar salad	pork chops	a glass of ice tea
clam chowder	oriental chicken	a bottle of imported beer
soup of the day	fish fillet	a cup of coffee
fried mushrooms	chicken pasta	some water

Restaurant Quiz

1. In speaking of meat, the opposite of tender is (soft, tough, fresh).
2. We generally fry things in a (dish, pan, bowl).
3. In a pound there are (12 ounces, 16 ounces, 20 ounces).

Lunch

Unit 5

Lunch

Unit 5

Lunch

Preview : Reading

▣ Selling Wine and Liquor

1. Basic Principles

You can learn a few basic principles about wine and liquor service that will make your job easier and more enjoyable. You can learn:

a) how to suggest the appropriate wine for your guest's entrée,
b) how to make a suggestion for before-dinner drinks that will increase sales,
c) the basic procedures for opening and serving wines

2. Wine and Foods

Red wines go well with hearty foods such as steak, roast duck, roast beef or pork chops.

White wines go well with light foods such as fish, seafood, light meats like veal, chicken, or turkey.

Champagne can be served with everything. However, if the guest requests white wine with the steak, let him have it.

3. Serving Temperature

Red wine: should be served at room temperature (65 degrees F, 18 degrees C)

White wine: all the white wines and sparkling wines are served chilled.

▣ Key Words

basic principle	기본원칙	temperature	온도
basic procedure	기본절차	go well with ~	~와 잘 어울리다
appropriate	적절한	degree	정도, 온도
increase	증가시키다	sparkling	포말성의
chill	차게 하다	entrée	주요리

▣ Reading Helper

1. 고객의 앙트레에 맞는 와인 권유방법

판매를 촉진시키는 식전 술 권유방법

와인 오프닝 및 서빙 절차

2. 요리 종류에 따라 서빙하는 와인의 종류도 다르다

적포도주 : 육류 / 백포도주: 생선, 가금류 / 샴페인: 모든 요리에 서빙

3. 서빙 온도도 중요

Red wine : 실내온도/ 65°F, 18℃

White wine / sparkling(포말성 와인)의 경우 냉각

Rose wine : 7~10℃

Sherry : 1~12℃

Champagne : 4~6℃

Basic Vocabulary

▣ Fill in the blank with the meaning in Korean.

broil	house wine
Fettuccine pasta	prawn
specials	curry

Key Expressions

▣ Make a full sentence using the words given in the bracket.

1. 점심 식사 주문할 준비가 되셨습니까?
   (lunch, order, ready, are, your, to, you, ?)

2. 무엇을 마시고 싶으십니까?
   (What, drink, would, to, like, you, ?)

3. 그것을 가지고 곧 바로 오겠습니다.
   (I'll, it, back, be, with, right)

4. 제가 주문을 받을까요?
(order, take, I, your, may, ?)

5. 오늘의 특별요리가 무엇입니까?
(specials, are, today's, what, ?)

6. 바에서 무엇을 좀 가져와도 될까요?
(May, something, I, the, bar, bring, from, ?)

7. 무엇을 추천하시겠습니까?
(do, recommend, what, you, ?)

8. 해물요리가 어떠세요?
(about, seafood, how, the, ?)

9. 업소 와인 한 잔 부탁드립니다.
(Let, house, me, glass, a, of, please, wine, order)

10. 당신의 음료수를 가지고 잠시 후 돌아오겠습니다.

(I'll, moment, a, with, be, in, back, drink, your)

Dialogues

Dialogue 1

W : Waitress G : Guest

W **Are you ready to order your lunch?**

G Yes. A hamburger, please.

W **What would you like to drink?**

G Do you have diet coke?

W No, we don't. We have diet 7-up, though.

G Then, a large diet 7-up with lots of ice.

W **I'll be right back with it.**

Notes

♠ Are you ready to order your lunch? 점심 주문하시겠어요?

♠ What would you like to drink? 무엇을 마시고 싶으세요?

♠ I'll be right back with it. 그것을 가지고 바로 다시 오겠습니다.

Dialogue 2

W : Waitress G : Guest

W Hello! **May I take your order?**

G1 Yes. **What are today's specials?**

W Our specials of the day are broiled salmon and Fettuccine pasta.

G1 I'll have the Fettuccine Pasta and my wife will have the broiled item.

W That is an excellent choice! May I bring something from the bar?

G1 Just water for me, please.

W And you, ma'am?

G2 I want a glass of house wine, please.

Notes

♠ May I take your order? 주문 받을까요?

♠ What are today's specials? 오늘의 특별요리는 무엇이지요?

♠ broiled salmon 구운 연어

♠ Fettuccine pasta 가죽끈모양 국수의 파스타

♠ Our specials of the day are a broiled salmon and Fettuccine pasta.
Today's specials
Chefs specials

♠ May I bring something from the bar? 바에서 뭘 좀 가져와도 될까요?
get you something from the bar
you something to drink

Dialogue 3

W: Waitress G: Guest

W Are you ready to order for your lunch?

G What do you recommend?

W How about the seafood? I believe the prawn curry is worth trying.

G OK. I'll take it.

W You are going to love your lunch. Would you like something to drink?

G **Let me order** a glass of house wine, please.

W Sounds great. I'll be back with your drink in a moment.

G Thanks a lot.

Notes

- ♠ What do you recommend? 무엇을 추천하시겠어요?
- ♠ How about the seafood? 해산물 요리가 어떠세요?
- ♠ prawn curry 참새우 카레
- ♠ Let me order a glass of house wine, please. 하우스와인 한잔 주문하겠습니다. (Grammar 부분 "Let me~" 설명 참조)

Grammar

1. Let me(verb)

Let me show you to your table, sir.
Let me order a glass of house wine, please.
Let me show you the menu.
Let me know your name.
Let me have the Fettuccine Pasta.

보기에서처럼 정중한 요청을 할 때에는 'Let me~' 로 시작한다.

2. Why don't you ~

> You should try some dessert.
> ➡ **Why don't you** try some dessert?

보기에서처럼 문장들을 매우 예의 바른 제안을 나타내는 "Why don't you"로 시작하는 문장으로 바꾸시오.

1) You should try some dessert.
   ➡ Why don't you try some dessert?

2) You ought to order a salad.
   ➡ ______________________________?

3) I recommend you to get the pasta.
   ➡ ______________________________?

4) You should drink some coffee.
   ➡ ______________________________?

5) I think you ought to have the steak.
   ➡ ______________________________?

6) I believe you should sample the wine.
   ➡ ______________________________?

Restaurant English Tips

▣ 칵테일을 위한 식사 도구들

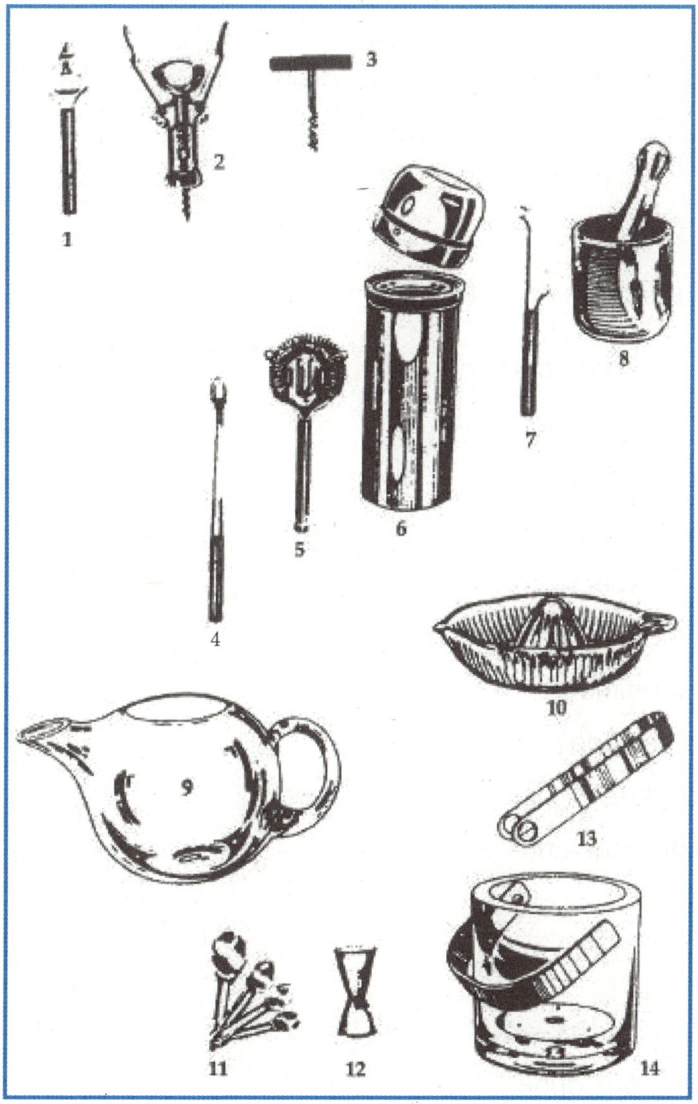

1 Bottle (can) opener

2 Corkscrew

3 Traditional corkscrew

4 Long spoon (bar spoon)

5 Bar – strainer with coil

6 Mixing glass (shaker 겸용)

7 Fruit peeling knife

8 Wooden muddler for mashing fruit or herbs

9 Water pitcher (large size)

10 Fruit juice squeezer

11 A set of measuring spoons

12 Jigger

13 Ice tongs

14 Ice bucket

Review & Exercises

1. Words to memorize in this unit

broil 굽다 (스테이크)
house wine 업소 와인
Fettuccine pasta 페투치네 파스타(가죽끈 모양의 파스타)
specials 특별요리
prawn 참새우
curry 카레

2. Key expressions to memorize in this unit

1. Are you ready to order your lunch?
2. What would you like to drink?
3. I'll be right back with it.
4. May I take your order?
5. What are today's specials?
6. May I bring something from the bar?
7. What do you recommend?
8. How about the seafood?
9. Let me order a glass of house wine, please.
10. I'll be back with your drink in a moment.

3. Exercises

1) Fill in the blank with the suitable preposition.

a. I'll be back with your drink ______ a moment.

b. Are you ready to order ______ your lunch?

c. May I bring something ______ the bar?

2) Pair Activity (1)

다음 예처럼 질문과 문장을 만든 다음 파트너와 연습하세요.

apple pie (cream or ice cream)

A : Can I have some apple pie, please?

B : Would you like it with cream or ice cream?

A : Ice cream, please.

(1)

coffee (milk or without)

A : Can I have some ______________, please?

B : Would you like it with ___________________?

A : ______________, please.

(2)

cheesecake (cream or ice cream)

A : Can I have some ______________, please?

B : Would you like it with ___________________?

A : ______________, please.

(3)

steak (French fries or salad)

A : Can I have some ______________, please?

B : Would you like it with ___________________?

A : ______________, please.

(4)

salad (French dressing or mayonnaise)

A : Can I have some ________, please?

B : Would you like it with __________?

A : ________, please.

3) Pair Activity (2)

아래 메뉴판을 보고 파트너와 함께 주문을 하고 또 주문을 받는 연습을 하세요.

MENU

APPETIZERS	
Stuffed Clams	$4.99
French Fries	$4.99
Onion Rings	$5.99
Mozzarella Sticks	$5.99
Potato Skins	$7.99
Entrée	
Chicken Parmiagiana with Spaghetti	$10.99
One-half Baked Chicken	$10.99
Grilled Pork Chops	$10.99
New York Strip Steak	$12.99
T-Bone Steak	$14.99

Waitress : Would you care for an appetizer before the main course?

Guest : Yes, I'd love to have some ________.

Waitress : That's a good choice. And how about the entrée?

Guest : I'll have the ________, please.

Restaurant Quiz

1. What food is the one that is economical, nutritious and easy to prepare?

   a) Eggs   b) Chicken   c) Beef-steak

2. The yolk is broken first, then turned over:

   a) Sunny-side up   b) Over-easy   c) Over-hard

3. The egg is gently turned over without breaking the yolk.

   a) Sunny-side up   b) Over-easy   c) Over-hard

4. It is done when the white is solid:

   a) Sunny-side up   b) Over-easy   c) Over-hard

나는
레스토랑 영어다

Dinner

Unit 6

Dinner

Unit 6

Dinner

Preview : Reading

▣ Table Setting

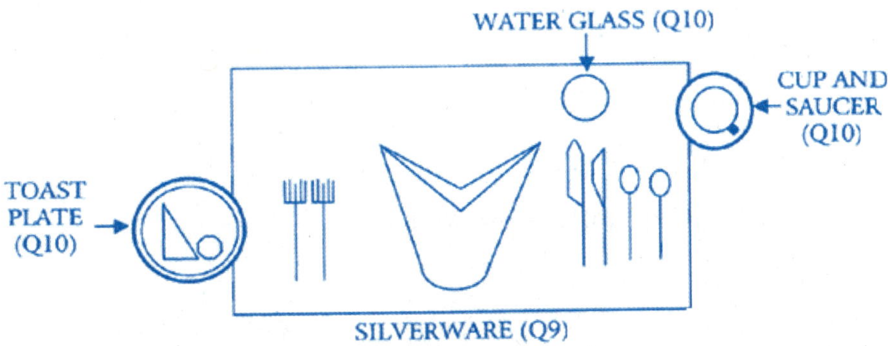

If you work as a waiter or waitress, you should know how to set the table.

1. You should lay out the table cloth or the place mats.
2. A general rule: items such as salt and pepper shakers are placed in the center of the table.
3. When picking up silverware, hold the pieces by their handles.

4. Forks, spoons, and knives are placed in the order of use. Forks on the left and next to the plate; knife edges facing the plate; handles of the silverware in a straight line and close to the table edge.
5. Hold plates by the edge. The bread and butter plate goes just above the forks. The glass goes just to the right of the tip of the dinner knife.
6. Other items go thus: Salad plate to the left. Cup and saucer to the right, handle within easy reach. Cream jug just above the cup and the service plate in the center.

▣ Key Words

table cloth	식탁보	plate	접시
place mat	1인용식기 깔개	saucer	받침접시
silverware	은식기	jug	단지
edge	모서리	service plate	큰접시

▣ Reading Helper

1. 테이블보와 식탁용 깔개 확인
2. 소금, 후추 셰이커 테이블 중앙에 위치
3. 은식기 집어들 때는 손잡이 잡기
4. 포크, 스푼, 나이프는 사용 순서에 따라 놓는다. 포크는 중앙에서 왼쪽에, 나이프는 오른쪽에, 칼날이 중앙을 향하도록. 은식기 손잡이 끝이 일직선이 되도록 테이블 가장자리 가까이 배치
5. 접시는 쥘 때에 가장자리 잡기/ 빵과 버터접시 포크 바로 위/ 물잔은 나이프 끝 오른쪽
6. 샐러드접시는 왼쪽/ 컵과 받침접시는 오른쪽/ 손잡이는 잡기 쉽도록 오른쪽을 향하도록/ 컵 위쪽에 크림 단지/ 큰 접시는 중앙에 위치

Basic Vocabulary

■ Fill in the blank with the meaning in Korean.

recommend	shrimp
fillet of sole	onion
poached	sirloin
salmon	goose
smoked	liver
lobster	Chablis
raw	pate
steamed	check
make up one's mind	grilled
	terrific

Key Expressions

■ Make a full sentence using the words given in the bracket.

1. 어떻게 준비하십니까?
(How, it, do, prepare, you, ?)

____

2. 스테이크를 어떻게 해드릴까요?
(steak, like, you, how, would, your, ?)

____

3. 당신은 그것에다가 수프 혹은 샐러드를 원하십니까?
(you, do, or, with, that, want, a soup, salad, ?)

____

4. 저는 야채 수프로 시작하고 싶어요.
(I'd, soup, the, start, to, with, vegetable, like)

____

5. 저는 결정을 할 수 없습니다.
(mind, up, can't, I, make, my)

____

6. 오늘 메뉴에 무엇이 좋습니까?
(menu, on, what's, today, good, the, ?)

____

7. 계산서 받을 수 있을까요?
(check, have, I, may, my, please, ?)

____

8. 음식을 추천해 주시겠어요?
(you, some, food, recommend, can, ?)

____

9. 어떤 수프를 드시고 싶으세요?

(would, like, you, which, to, have, soup, ?)

---

10. 주요리(앙트레)로 당신의 특별요리는 무엇입니까?

(What, entrée, is, for, your, specialty, an, ?)

Dialogues

Dialogue 1

W : Waitress G : Guest

W Good evening, sir! This is today's menu.

G Any special recommendations, captain.

W We have fresh sole from the market. May I suggest **fillet of sole** poached in chablis, sir? It is the most popular dish from our menu.

G It sounds fascinating. **How do you prepare it?**

W It is poached sole, accompanied by mashed potatoes. It is very tasty.

G Sounds **terrific** and just to my taste! All right, I'll have that.

W Yes, sir. Would you care for an appetizer? Our home-made **pate** or perhaps some other appetizer?

Notes

♠ fillet of sole 서대기 저민 살코기

♠ How do you prepare it? 어떻게 준비하세요?
♠ terrific 굉장한
♠ pate 머리, 고기파이

Dialogue 2

W : Waiter G : Guest

W Three orders of sirloin steak? How would you like your steak?

G Let's see. Two well-done, and one medium-rare, please.

W Okay. Do you want a soup or salad with that?

G What's today's soup?

W It's cream of mushroom. It's really good.

G I'll have that. It looks like all of us will have the soup.

W And would you like something to drink?

G Yes. We'll have a bottle of table wine.

Notes

♠ How would like your steak? 스테이크를 어떻게 해드릴까요?
♠ Do you want a soup or salad with that? 그것과 함께 수프 혹은 샐러드를 원하세요?

Dialogue 3

W : Waitress G : Guest

W Good evening. May I take your order?

G Yes, please.

W What would you like?

G I'd like to start with the vegetable soup.

W All right. And what about your main course?

G Broiled lobster with a salad.

W Sounds good, sir. Please allow me to repeat your order. You've ordered the vegetable soup and lobster with a salad as main course. Is that correct?

G Right.

Notes

♠ I'd like to start with the vegetable soup.
begin with the vegetable soup
have the vegetable soup as a starter

♠ Please allow me to repeat your order. 주문하신 것을 반복해보겠습니다.

Dialogue 4

W : Waiter G : Guest

G I can't make up my mind. Everything is so good.

W If you are considering fish, I'll recommend the grilled salmon.

G Does it come with salad?

W Yes, it does.

G OK I'll take it.

Notes

♠ I can't make up my mind. 제가 결정할 수가 없군요.

♠ Does it come with salad? 그것은 샐러드와 함께 나오나요?
soup

Dialogue 5

W : Waitress G : Guest

W Good evening, sir. May I take your order?

G Yes, What's good on the menu today?

W We are selling a lot of sole and flounder tonight. We have them baked or broiled.

G I'm not too strong on fish. I'll just have a medium rare steak.

W Yes, sir. Would you like a baked potato or French fries?

G A baked sweet potato with honey butter and Balsamic dressing on the salad.

W Thank you for your order.

Dialogue 6

W : Waitress G : Guest

W Good evening, sir. May I take your order, please?

G1 Bring each of us a **shrimp cocktail.** Then I want the **broiled lobster** with French fries, Italian dressing on my salad. Then my wife wants baked chicken with **mashed potatoes, Thousand island dressing** on her salad.

W How would you like your steak?

G1 I want my steak medium rare with baked potatoes. My wife wants her chicken well done, baked potatoes with butter.

W What would you like to drink?

G1 A cup of coffee, please.

G2 Tea with milk, please.

W What would you like for dessert now, sir?

G1 Apple pie, please.

G2 Strawberry ice cream.

W Very well, sir and ma'am.

G1 Waitress, **may I have my check,** please?

W Here you are, sir. Please pay the cashier on your way out.

Notes

- shrimp cocktail : 새우 칵테일
- broiled lobster : 불에 직접 구운 바다가재
- dressing : 드레싱. 샐러드, 육류, 생선 따위에 치는 일종의 소스
- Italian dressing : 식초와 기름을 바탕으로 마늘, 양파 등의 맛을 곁들인 것
- Thousand island dressing : 마요네즈에 파슬리, 피클수, 피망, 삶은 달걀, 케찹 등을 다져서 첨가한 것
- French dressing : 기름, 식초, 레몬즙, 겨자, 파프리카(일종의 고추) 등으로 만든 드레싱
- mashed potatoes : 으깬 감자
- check (=bill) : 계산서 May I have my **check,** please? 계산서 좀 주시겠어요?

Dialogue 7

S : Server G : Guest

S Good evening. Here is the menu

G **Can you recommend some food?**

S For an appetizer, we're serving smoked salmon and shrimp cocktail with grapefruit.

G I'd like to have the shrimp cocktail, please.

S Very well, sir. Which soup would you like to have?

G Onion soup, please.

S All right.

G What is your specialty for an entrée?

S Today, we have the sirloin steak with goose liver or lobster with lemon sauce.

G I'll take the sirloin steak.

S How would you like to have it, sir?

G Medium-well done, please.

S OK, thanks. We've a choice of French, Thousand Island, and Italian dressing. Which one would you prefer?

G Thousand Island, please.

S All right, sir. Wait a second, please. We will serve it right away.

Notes

- ♠ Can you recommend some food? 음식을 추천하시겠어요?
- ♠ Which soup would you like to have? 어떤 수프를 드시고 싶으세요?
- ♠ What is your specialty for an entrée? 주요리로 특기가 무엇이죠?
- ♠ sirloin steak 등심 스테이크
- ♠ goose liver 거위 간

Dialogue 8

S : Server G : Guest

S Good evening. May I take your order?

G Can you recommend something special?

S Is this your first trying of Japanese food?

G No, I have eaten before but I don't know it well. I just tried Sushi twice.

S The set menu is a good introduction to Japanese food. If you want to taste a variety of Japanese food, I recommend either the Sashimi set menu or the Tempura set menu.

G What does the Sashimi set menu include?

S It includes raw fish, steamed rice, miso soup, Japanese pickle and fruit.

G I will try the Sashimi set.

S Thank you very much. The Sashimi set is the most popular dish. You will be satisfied with it. If you need anything else, please let me know.

G Thank you.

Notes

♠ trying (=trial, 시도)

♠ be satisfied with ~에 만족하다

Grammar

▣ 수동태 구문

> The chef makes ice cream from cream, eggs, and sugar.
> ➡ Ice cream is made from cream, eggs, and sugar.

1. 어떻게 음식이 만들어지는가를 표현할 때 수동태가 자주 사용된다. 위 보기에서처럼 정확한 수동태로 문장을 만드시오.

 1) We make pasta from flour, eggs, and salt.

 ➡ ______________________________

 2) We make dressing from oil and vinegar.

 ➡ ______________________________

2. 테이블 세팅 과정을 표현하는 문장에서도 수동태가 흔히 등장한다. 다음 보기처럼 수동태 문장을 만드시오.

> table / lay / in the evening
> ➡ The table is laid in the evening.

 1) tablecloth / place / on the table

 ➡ ______________________________

 2) napkin / fold and place / on the side plate

 ➡ ______________________________

3) knife and fork / place / each side of the plate

➡ ____

4) wine glass / put / above the soup spoon

➡ ____

5) salt and pepper / put / in the middle of the table

➡ ____

6) main course plate / take away / when the main course is finished

➡ ____

7) dessert spoon and fork / bring/ with the dessert menu

➡ ____

8) flower arrangement / place / next to the salt and pepper.

➡ ____

Restaurant English Tips

1 요리의 종류

1) á la carte : 일품요리, 주문식단

2) table d'hote : 정식

(appetizer → soup → fish → main dish → salad → dessert → beverage)

3) set menu : 미리 메뉴가 정해져 세트당 가격이 책정됨.

2 Table Setting

1 napkin ( )	7 first course fork ( )
2 side plate ( )	8 soup spoon ( )
3 butter knife ( )	9 wine glass ( )
4 main course knife ( )	10 salt and pepper ( )
5 main course fork ( )	11 fish knife and fork ( )
6 first course knife ( )	12 dessert spoon and fork ( )

Review & Exercises

1. Words to memorize in this unit

recommend 추천하다
fillet of sole 서대기 저민살
poached 수란의
salmon 연어
smoked 훈제
shrimp 새우
chablis 샤블리, 프랑스 브르고뉴 지방에서 생산되는 화이트와인
lobster 바닷가재
raw 날것의
steamed 찐
pate 머리, 고기파이

onion 양파
sirloin 등심
goose 거위
liver 간
make up one's mind 결정하다
grilled 석쇠에 구운
terrific 굉장한
check 계산서

2. Key expressions to memorize in this unit

1. How do you prepare it?
2. How would you like your steak?
3. Do you want a soup or salad with that?
4. I'd like to start with the vegetable soup.
5. I can't make up my mind.
6. What's good on the menu today?
7. May I have my check, please?
8. Can you recommend some food?
9. Which soup would you like to have?
10. What is your specialty for an entrée?

3. Exercises

1) Fill in the blank with the suitable preposition.

a. I'd like to start ______ the vegetable soup.
b. Please allow me ______ repeat your order.
c. I can't make ______ my mind.
d. What's good ______ the menu today?

2) Pair Activity (1)

Fill in the blanks and practice with your partner.

S : Good evening. Here ______________________.

(여기 메뉴 있습니다)

G : Can you ______________________________?

(음식을 추천해 줄 수 있으세요?)

S : For an appetizer, we're serving smoked salmon and __________ ____________ with grape fruit.

(애프타이저로 우리는 훈제연어와 자몽과 함께 새우 칵테일을 제공합니다)

G : I'd like to ____________________, please.

(저는 새우칵테일로 주세요)

S : Very well, sir. Which soup would you _____________________?

(어떤 수프를 드시고 싶으세요?)

G : Onion soup, please.

S : All right

G: What is your ______________________ an entrée?

(앙트레로서 당신의 특별요리가 무엇입니까?)

S : Today, we have sirloin steak with goose liver or lobster with lemon sauce.

G : I'll take sirloin steak.

S : How would you ______________________, sir?

(어떻게 드시고 싶으세요?)

G : Medium-well done, please.

S : O.K, thanks. We've a choice of French, Thousand Island and Italian dressing. Which one _______________________?

(어느 것을 선호하세요?)

G : Thousand Island, please

S: All right sir. ________________________, please.

(잠깐만 기다려주세요)

We will serve it right away.

3) Pair Activity (2)

Practice the conversation with your partner. Use the information in the box below.

A : How are you enjoying your meal? Can I interest you in ________?

B : Well, I've already eaten a lot. I probably shouldn't order anything else.

A : Why don't you try ________________. It's ________________.

B : It sounds wonderful. Yes, I think that I'll try that.

A : I'll be back with it in just a couple of minutes.

B : Could you bring the check with you, too? I'd like to pay my bill.

A : Yes, I'll bring that to you in a moment.

Type of Food or Drink	Name of Food or Drink	Description of Food or Drink
an after-dinner drink	an Irish coffee	nice and strong
some wine	some port wine	rich and smooth
a cocktail	a brandy Alexander	sweet
some beer	some dark beer	imported

Restaurant Quiz

1. The first principle of order-taking is to (know how to set up the table, know how to greet guests, know the menu).
2. When you know your menu well, you are better able to (know the day's special, talk to the chef, help your guest order).

나는 레스토랑 영어다

Beverage & Dessert

Unit 7

Beverage & Dessert

Unit 7

Beverage & Dessert

호텔 음료 부서는 고객에게 음료 및 음료 서비스를 제공함으로써 고객의 요구를 충족한다. 음료에는 알콜 음료와 비알콜 음료로 구분하는데 특히 와인과 맥주에 대한 지식을 숙지하는 것이 중요하다.

Preview : Reading

▣ Typical Korean Foods and Drinks

1. Korean Meals

Korean meals basically consist of boiled rice and soups together with many side dishes. We often have fish or meat cooked in various ways.

2. Kimchi

Pickled vegetables (cabbage or radish) spiced with hot red pepper, garlic, ginger, and so on. It's served with every meal.

3. Bulgogi

Thin slices of beef that you broil over a charcoal fire at your table. Korean people like to eat it wrapped in a raw lettuce, while drinking beer or soju.

4. Soju

A kind of liquor distilled from various kinds of cereals. It is very popular among Korean people. It is as pure and clear as water and is about 60 proof.

5. Makkolli

A traditional Korean wine made from fermented rice or wheat. Almost every peasant family knows how to brew it, and it is an indispensable drink for the farmers working in the fields.

6. Naeng Myon

Tough noodles served in a bowl with spicy hot red pepper and mustard. Koreans enjoy it especially in the summer, since it is so refreshing.

▣ Key Words

basically	근본적으로	liquor	액체
side dishes	반찬	distil	증류하다
pickle	절이다	proof	알코올농도(퍼센트의 반)
cabbage	배추	ferment	발효시키다
radish	무	wheat	밀

spice	양념	peasant	농가
red pepper	고추	brew	양조하다
garlic	마늘	indispensable	필수불가결한
ginger	생강	rib	갈비
slice	조각	braise	낮은 열로 조림하다
charcoal	숯불	tough	질긴, 거친
broil	굽다	spicy	매운
wrap	싸다	mustard	겨자
raw	날 것	refreshing	상쾌한
lettuce	상치		

▣ Reading Helper

1. 한국식사의 기본구성 : 쌀밥과 국, 반찬/ 생선, 육류
2. 김치 : 소금에 절인 배추, 무, 양념, 고추, 마늘, 생강
3. 불고기 : 얇게 저민 쇠고기/ 테이블에서 숯불에 굽고 상치에 싸서 먹음.
4. 소주 : 맑은 물같은 곡류 증류주/ 60 proof

▶ proof와 퍼센트

퍼센트 : % = ml = 도(度)

옛날 영국에서 발효시켜 만든 술을 증류하여 알코올을 얻을 수 있다는 것을 알았지만 측정하는 방법이 없었다. 그래서 생각해낸 것이 알코올에 화약을 섞어 불을 붙여 붙으면 'proof!'라고 외침. 증류가 잘된 고농도 알코올이란 뜻, 즉 물을 타지 않은 술로 '증명'이 되는 것. 이때 불꽃이 일어나는 시점을 '100 proof'라고 했는데 이것은 농도가 대략 50%, 50도.

5. 막걸리 : 한국의 전통와인(쌀, 밀 발효) / 농가마다 양조법 알고 있다 / 농부들의 필수 전통주
6. 냉면 : 큰 사발, 질긴 면 / 겨자, 고추양념 / 차갑고 상쾌한 맛

Basic Vocabulary

▣ Fill in the blank with the meaning in Korean.

fat free	mustard
a la mode	B.L.T. sandwich
decaffeinated	on the rocks
veggie	

Key Expressions

▣ Make a full sentence using the words given in the bracket.

1. 그 밖에 다른 것 갖다 드릴까요?
(Can, else, you, I, get, anything, ?)

____

2 식사 전에 마실 것 좀 드시겠어요?
(you, would, like, before, something, meal, to drink, your, ?)

____

3. 뭔가 인기 있는 것을 추천해 주시겠어요?
(popular, recommend, would, something, you, ?)

____

4. 당신의 선택에 도움 드릴까요?
(Can, help, with, I, you, your choice, ?)

____

5. 여유있게 하세요.
(time, take, your)

____

6. 그것이 여기서 드실 겁니까 아니면 갖고 가실 거에요?
(go, or, for, that, will, be, here, to, ma'am, ?)

____

7. 제가 주문한 것 좀 서둘러주시겠어요?
(rush, my, you, please, order, will, ?)

____

8. 마실 것 좀 주문하시겠어요?
(would, to, like, something, order, drink, you, to, ?)

____

9. 어떤 종류의 드레싱을 드시고 싶으세요?
(dressing, kind, would, of, what, have, to, you, like, ?)

____

10. 그 밖에 다른 것 좀 하시겠어요?
(else, like, would, you, anything, ?)

____

Dialogues

Dialogue 1

W : Waiter G : Guest

W Many people like chocolate mousse. It's delicious.

G That's just too much for me.

W Well, we have some nice **fat free** ice creams, though. Straw-berry, vanilla, and mango.

G I'll try mango.

W OK. Can I bring you some coffee with that?

G Yes, a cup of capuccino, please.

Notes

♠ fat free 기름기를 뺀

Dialogue 2

W : Waiter G : Guest

W **Can I get you anything else?**

G No, thanks. It was delicious.
But I've already eaten too much.

W Can I offer you **another cup of coffee?**

G Yes, please. I'd love some.

Notes

♠ Can I get you anything else? 다른 것 더 드릴까요?

♠ another cup of coffee? 커피 한잔 더 드실래요?

Dialogue 3

W : Waiter G : Guest

W Good evening, sir. Would you like something to drink before your meal?

G Let me have a dry Martini, please.

W How would you like it, sir?

G Two ounces of gin to one of dry Vermouth on crushed ice.

W What brand of gin would you like?

G It doesn't matter. Whatever you have is O.K.

Notes

♠ Would you like something to drink before your meal? 식전에 마실 것 좀 드시겠어요?

♠ crushed 잘게 부순

Dialogue 4

W : Waiter G : Guest

W Have you enjoyed your meal?

G Yes, I had a great time. What type of dessert do you have in your restaurant?

W I'll bring the dessert list.

G Would you recommend something popular?

W Many people prefer Strawberry Bottom Pie. It's very delicious.

G I've already had it before. I'll try different one.

W Well, how about an apple pie a la mode.

G I'll try it.

W OK. Could I bring you some coffee with that?

G Yes, a cup of coffee, please.

Notes

♠ Would you recommend something popular? 인기 있는 것 추천해 주시겠어요?

♠ an apple pie with a la mode 아이스크림을 얹은 애플파이

Dialogue 5

W : Waiter G : Guest

W Did you enjoy your stay? Anything else to need?

G No. It was perfect. Thank you for your assistance.

W What kind of dessert do you like?

G It's not easy to choose the menu.

W Then, **can I help you with your choice?**

G Thanks. What is the popular one in your restaurant?

W I'd recommend Death by Chocolate.

G OK. I'll take it.

Notes

♠ Can I help you with your choice? 당신의 선택에 도와드릴까요?

Dialogue 6

W : Waiter G : Guest

W May I show you our dessert menu?

G Yes, please.

W **Take your time.** I'll be back to take your order.

G Can I have some more coke?

W Haven't you decided yet?

G Yes, **one scoop of** vanilla ice cream.

W Would you like coffee with that?

G Yes, thanks.

Notes

♠ take your time. 손님이 아직 준비 안되었을 때 서둘지말라고 하는 말, 재촉하거나 참을성 없는 인상을 주면 안된다.

♠ one scoop of 한 국자의

Dialogue 7

W : Waiter G : Guest

W Would you like coffee, madam?

G Do you have any decaffeinated coffee?

W Yes, we do. Regular, Brazilian special **blend** and espresso.

G Regular for me.

W How do you take it?

G Black. With sugar, please.

W And for you, sir?

G No, thanks.

Notes

♠ blend 혼합한 것

Dialogue 8

C : Counter Server G : Guest

C May I help you, ma'am?

G Yes, I'd like a BIG Mac, a Fish Mac, three large French fries and three regular cokes, please.

C Is that all?

G Yes, that's it.

C That'll be $6.80, please. **Will that be for here or to go,** ma'am?

G To eat here, please.

Notes

♠ Will that be for here or to go? 여기서 드실 겁니까 아니면 가지고 가실 겁니까?

Dialogue 9

C : Counter Server G : Guest

C What will it be?

G Two **veggie** burgers to take out, please.

C With ketchup, mayonnaise, or mustard?

G Ketchup, please.

G Something to drink?

C No, thanks. Will you please rush my order? I'm in a hurry.

G They'll be ready in a minute.

Notes

- veggie 채식주의자
- rush my order 주문한 것을 서두르다

Dialogue 10

C : Counter Server G : Guest

C Are you ready to order, sir?

G Yes, I'll have a B.L.T. sandwich.

C Would you like to order something to drink?

G Yes, let me have a large coke.

Notes

- B.L.T sandwich Bacon, Lettuce, Tomato로 구성된 샌드위치
- Are you ready to order, sir?
  = May I take tour order?
  = What will you have today?
  = Have you decided?
- Would you like to order something to drink? 마실 것 좀 드시겠어요?

Dialogue 11

W : Waitress G : Guest

W Good evening. What can I get for you?

G1 A double whiskey, please.

W And what's your pleasure, sir?

G2 Get me a scotch **on the rocks.**

W Sure.

Notes

♠ on the rocks 얼음을 띄운

Dialogue 12

W : Waiter G : Guest

G The same again, please.

W It's coming right up.

(a little later)

W Here you are, and here are some crisps on the house.

G Thanks.

Dialogue 13

S : Server G : Guest

S Can I take your order now?

G Could you bring me a glass of beer while I'm deciding?

S Yes, sir. Are you ready, sir?

G Yes, I'd like some beef curry with rice.

S OK. It comes with salad. **What kind of dressing would you like to have?**

G Italian dressing, please.

S **Would you like anything else?**

G I'd like to have watermelon as a dessert.

Notes

♠ What kind of dressing would you like to have? 어떤 드레싱을 하시겠어요?

♠ Would you like anything else? 그밖에 다른 것을 원하세요?

Grammar

1. Some/Any

보통 평서문에서는 some을 사용하고 의문과 부정적 표현에서는 any를 사용하나, 예의바른 제안과 요청 문장에서는 의문문일지라도 some을 사용한다.

I'd like **some** ice cream.

Would you like **some** more wine?

Can we have **some** bread, please?

다음 문장을 some 또는 any로 채우시오.

1) Do you have ________ fresh fruit?

2) Could we have ________ water, please?

3) Would you like ________ coffee?

4) I'm sorry, we don't have ________ fresh fish today.

5) Can I get you ________ more drinks?

6) There isn't ________ cheese.

2. Can you ~? / Could you ~?

어떤 일을 요청할 때에 다음 예처럼 Can you 혹은 Could you로 시작하는 경우가 많다.

> **Can you** bring us a bottle of water, please?
> **Could you** change mine, please?

위 보기처럼 괄호 안에 주어진 동사를 사용하여 적어보시오.

1) You don't know the telephone number of a caller. (give)

____?

2) You didn't hear a customer's surname. (repeat)

____?

3) You don't know how to spell the name of a town. (spell)

____?

4) You want to know if there are any vegetarians in a group. (tell)

____?

5) You are not sure what time a guest is arriving. (confirm)

____?

6) You want to check how many people there are in a group. (tell)

____?

Restaurant English Tips

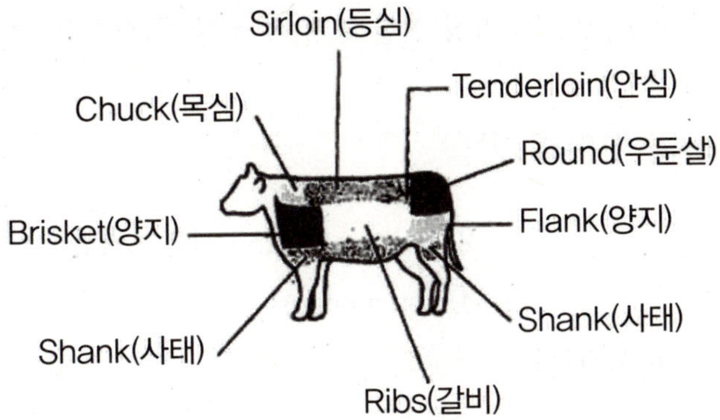

▣ 쇠고기(beef)

brisket 양짓살
shank 사태
striploin 채끝
grain-fed 곡물을 먹여 키운
grass-fed 풀을 먹여 키운
grass-fed beef 풀을 먹여 키운 소
breast-fed 엄마젖으로 키운
milk-fed 우유로 키운
veal 송아지고기
chuck 목심(어깨살)
loin 등심, 안심
sirloin 등심
tenderloin 안심
round 우둔살
rib 갈비
flank 양짓살

▣ porterhouse

허리고기 윗부분 살에서 안심(tenderloin)과 T-bone 뼈를 갈아 잘라낸 큰 스테이크

▣ ribs 갈비부분

1) porterhouse steak　　　2) T-bone steak

3) rib steak(prime ribs, short ribs)

▣ tenderloin

안심, 소, 돼지 허리 부분의 가장 연한 고기, 갈비살 아래에 위치한다.

▣ Tenderloin의 부분별 명칭

1) tete 머리부분　　　2) chateaubriand 샤또브리앙

3) fillet　　　4) tournedoes

5) fillet mignon 꼬리부분

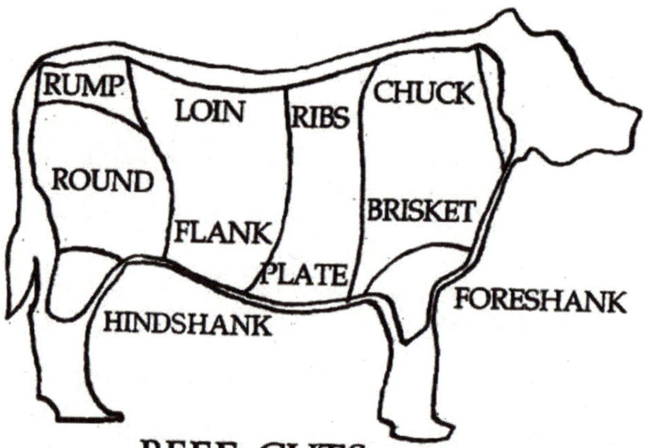

BEEF CUTS

Review & Exercises

1. Words to memorize in this unit

fat free 기름기를 뺀

a la mode 아이스크림을 얹은

decaffeinated 카페인을 뺀

veggie 채식주의자

mustard 겨자

BLT sandwich Bacon, Lettuce, Tomato 샌드위치

on the rocks 얼음을 띄운

2. Key expressions to memorize in this unit

1. Can I get you anything else?
2. Would you like something to drink before your meal?
3. Would you recommend something popular?
4. Can I help you with your choice?
5. Take your time.
6. Will that be for here or to go, ma'am?
7. Will you please rush my order?
8. Would you like to order something to drink?
9. What kind of dressing would you like to have?
10. Would you like anything else?

3. Exercises

1) Fill in the blank with the suitable preposition.

a. Can I help you ______ your choice?

b. Will that be for here or ______ go, ma'am?

c. I'm ______ a hurry.

d. Get me a scotch ______ the rocks.

2) Pair Activity

(1) 다음 대화에서 웨이터 부분을 주어진 단어를 사용하여 완성하고 파트너와 연습하세요.

W : (All right?)

G : Yes, thanks. Delicious.

W : (Dessert?)

G : Hazelnut gâteau for me, I think.

W : (Coffee?)

G : Yes, thanks. That would be nice.

(2) Pair Activity

Look at the menu. Then complete the check and the conversation.

Waitress : Are you ready to order?

Customer : Yes. I'd like a ______________ and ______________.

Waitress : OK. Anything to drink?

Customer : ____________________, please.

(Later)

Waitress : Can I get you anything else?

Customer : I'd like __________ piece of ___________, please. Oh, and I'd like ____________ chocolate __________, too. And _____________, please.

Restaurant Quiz

1. You can influence your guest's choice by using terms suggesting that the selection is a specialty of the house. Which of the following terms are most appropriate for suggestive selling? Which of the following terms are good for suggestive selling?

   a) Everybody's favorite b) Our chef's choice
   c) Well-known d) Our specialty
   e) Homemade

2. Which wine would you recommend with each of the following?

   a) Any entrée 1) Red wine
   b) Fish 2) White wine
   c) Roast beef 3) Rose or champagne

Chapter 3

More on Restaurant Services

나는 레스토랑 영어다

Unit 8

Handling Complaints

Unit 8

Handling Complaints

Preview : Reading

▣ The Korean Foods

1. Bibimbap (Rice Mixed with vegetables and Beef)

Bibimbap is one of Korea's most well-known dishes. It is both delicious and nutritious. Regions throughout the Korean Peninsula have their own unique versions of bibimbap, but the most famous is the one from Jeonju-si in Jeollabukdo.

2. Jeon (Korean pancake)

Better known as "Korean pancake" Jeon is popular among tourists. In Korea, people enjoy eating Jeon on rainy days. Especially popular are phajeon (green onion pancake), and kimchijeon (kimchi pancake).

3. Samgyeopsal (Grilled pork Belly)

Samgyeopsal is a cut of pork belly meat whose name literally translates to three-layered meat. Slices of samgyeopsal are typically char-grilled or cooked in a pan, then wrapped in lettuce or sesame leaf with garlic and ssamjang (soybean dipping sauce). The best accompaniment to samgyeopsal is none other than Korea's famous alcohol, Soju.

4. Samgyetang (Ginseng chicken soup)

There is a strong belief in Korea that the body's energy must be replenished during the hot months of summer. Therefore when the heat of summer is at its peak, many people will eat Samgyetang, or chicken ginseng soup. Samgyetang is made by stuffing a small hen with ginseng, glutinous rice, garlic, jujubes and chestnuts, then slow-cooking the ingredients until the meat is tender.

▣ Key Words

nutritious	영양가 많은	belief	믿음, 신념
Korean Peninsula	한반도	replenish	강화하다
unique	독특한	ginseng	인삼
literally	문자 그대로	stuff	쑤셔넣다
translate	번역하다	glutinous rice	찹쌀
belly	뱃살	jujube	대추
three-layered	세 겹의	chestnut	밤
char-grilled	숯불에 구운	ingredient	재료
sesame leaf	깻잎	tender	부드러운
none other than	다름 아닌	soybean	간장

▣ Reading Helper

1. 비빔밥 (야채 고기 밥) : 맛있는 영양식, 전주비빔밥
2. 전 (한국 팬케익) : 비오는 날 인기, 파전, 김치전

3. 삼겹살 (숯불 돼지고기) : 삼겹, 마늘, 쌈장, 깻잎, 소주

4. 삼계탕 (인삼 닭고기 스프) : 여름 체력 증강용, 인삼, 찹쌀, 마늘, 대추, 밤

Basic Vocabulary

▣ Fill in the blank with the meaning in Korean.

overdone	awfully
tough	favor
apologize	sodium

Key Expressions

▣ Make a full sentence using the words given in the bracket.

1. 이것은 제가 주문한 것이 아닙니다.
(what, ordered, not, is, this, I)

____

2. 기다리시는 동안에 다른 어떤 것을 드시겠습니까?
(would, something else, like, you, while, waiting, are, you, ?)

____

3. 주문하신 것이 섞인 것 같습니다.
(I' m, got, afraid, the orders, mixed up)

____

4. 모든 상황이 괜찮습니까 선생님?
(everything, sir, is, all right, ?)

____

5. 조금 더 익혀 드리면 좋겠습니까?
(like, would, it, you, more, cooked, a little, ?)

____

6. 저는 아직도 서빙 받지 못했습니다.
(I, yet, been, haven't, served)

____

7. 기다리시게 해서 죄송합니다 선생님
(kept, waiting, have, sorry, I'm, you, to, sir)

____

8. 저를 위해 그것을 교환해 주시겠습니까?
(would, me, it, for, exchange, you, ?)

____

9. 부탁 하나 드려도 될까요?
(will, me, a favor, you, do, ?)

____

10. 저는 저염식 식이요법을 하고 있는 중입니다.
(I'm, diet, low, a, on, sodium)

____

Dialogues

Dialogue 1

S : Server G : Guest

G This is not what I ordered. I said I wanted a cheeseburger. This looks like a ham and cheese sandwich to me.

S I'm sorry, sir, I'll send it back. Would you like something else while you are waiting?

G Yes. Give me another Martini.

Notes

♠ This is not what I ordered. 이것은 제가 주문한 것이 아닙니다.
what I asked for
what I wanted

Dialogue 2

W : Waiter G : Guest

G Excuse me. Waiter!

W Yes, ma'am?

G This is not what I ordered. I asked for Thousand Island dressing, not Blue cheese.

W I'm so sorry, ma'am. I'm afraid the orders got mixed up. I'll get you another salad right away.

Notes

♠ ask for 요구하다 (= demand)
♠ I'm afraid the orders got mixed up. 주문들이 섞인 것 같습니다.

Dialogue 3

W : Waitress G : Guest

G Waitress!

W Yes, sir?

G This meat's overdone! I told you I wanted it rare! And I'm sorry to say this. but it's **as tough as leather.**

W I'm terribly sorry, sir. I'll send it back.

G Can you recommend something else?

Notes

♠ as tough as leather 가죽처럼 질긴

Dialogue 4

W : Waitress G : Guest

G Waitress!

W **Is everything all right, sir?**

G Not exactly. This steak is raw. I asked for it well done! And it's rather cold.

W I **do apologize,** sir. **Would you like it cooked a little more?**

G Please.

W **Would you like something else while you're waiting?**

G No, thank you. but tell them to hurry.

Notes

♠ Is everything all right, sir? 모든 게 다 괜찮으세요?

♠ I do apologize. 정말 사과드려요. (do는 강조의 뜻)

♠ Would you like it cooked a little more? 조금 더 요리해 드릴까요?

♠ Would you like something else while you're waiting? 기다리시는 동안에 다른 것 좀 드시겠어요?

Dialogue 5

W : Waitress G : Guest

G Excuse me, **I haven't been served yet.** Why is it taking so long?

W **I'm sorry to have kept you waiting, sir.** And I'll go to check with the kitchen and find out what's taking so long.

(A little later)

G Hello? This is not what I ordered.

W **I'm awfully sorry.** What's the problem, sir?

G I ordered the chicken entrée but the server brought me fish. **Would you exchange it for me?**

W Why certainly! Let me take this and I'll bring your order to you.

G Be sure to bring the right one.

W Pardon me for the mix-up. I'll double check on your order.

Notes

♠ I haven't been served yet. 저는 아직도 음식서비스를 받지 못했어요.

♠ I'm sorry to have kept you waiting, sir. 기다리게 해 드려서 죄송합니다.

♠ I'm awfully sorry. 정말 죄송합니다. (awfully 지독하게, 매우)

♠ Would you exchange it for me? 저를 위해 좀 바꾸어주시겠어요?

Dialogue 6

W : Waitress G : Guest

G Waitress, I haven't been served yet!

W Wait a moment. sir. And I'll take care of you.

(A little later)

G This isn't what I ordered.

I ordered the New York steak. This is fish.

W I'm awfully sorry. I'll change it soon.

Dialogue 7

W : Waiter G : Guest

G Excuse me. **Will you do me a favor? I didn't know salmon is on the entrée.** I don't like fish. Can I have chicken **instead of** fish?

W I'll talk to the manager, ma'am. I'll see if we can arrange that.

G Oh, thanks.

W You're welcome

Notes

♠ Will you do me a favor? 제게 호의 좀 베풀어주실래요? 제가 부탁 좀 드려도 될까요? (favor 호의)

♠ I didn't know salmon is on the entrée 앙트레에 연어가 들어있는 줄 몰랐어요
pork
chicken

♠ instead of ~ 대신에

Dialogue 8

W : Waitress G : Guest

G Hey! **I'm on a low sodium diet.** Can you find out the salt content for me?

W OK. I'll check with the chef to see how much salt is in it.

(after a while)

W Sir. **It's prepared with low sodium.**

G Thank you.

W Not at all.

Notes

♠ I'm on a low sodium diet. 저는 저염식 다이어트를 하고 있어요

♠ It's prepared with low sodium 그것은 저염식으로 준비됩니다.
without sugar (무과당으로)
without MSG (조미료 없이)

♠ MSG(MonoSodium Glutamate 글루탐산 나트륨)

Grammar

▣ I'll get ~

"I'll get you some."에서처럼 "I'll + verb"는 뭔가를 제공할 때 하는 표현이다.

A I'd like a map B I'll get (you) one.	A This spoon is dirty. B I'll get you another.
A I'd like some bread. B I'll bring (you) some....	A There isn't any bread left. B I'll order (you) some more.

아래 보기처럼 괄호 안에 주어진 표현을 사용하여 대화를 완성하여 보세요.

> A : Could we have some bread? (get / some)
> B : Yes. I'll get (you) some.

1) A : Can I have an orange juice, please? (get / one)
   B : ______________________________.

2) A : Our water jug is empty. (get / some more)
   B : ______________________________.

3) A : This bottle of wine is corked. (bring / another)
   B : ______________________________.

4) A : Could I have a beer, please? (get / one)
   B : ______________________________.

5) A : This fork is dirty. (bring / another)
   B : ______________________________.

Restaurant English Tips

▣ 닭고기(Chicken)

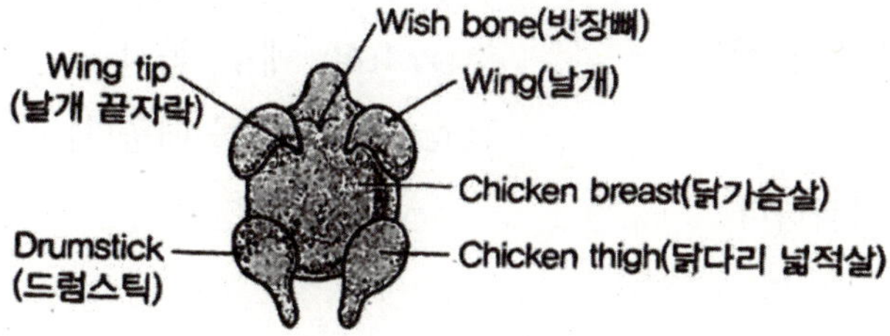

가금류(poultry)

chicken breast 닭가슴살
drumstick 드럼스틱
wing 날개
wing tip 날개 끝자락
wish bone 빗장뼈
neck 목
thigh 다리살(허벅지)

pheasant 꿩
quail 메추리
pigeon 비둘기
duck 오리
goose 거위
turkey 칠면조
free range chicken 방목해 키운 닭

▣ 돼지고기(pork)

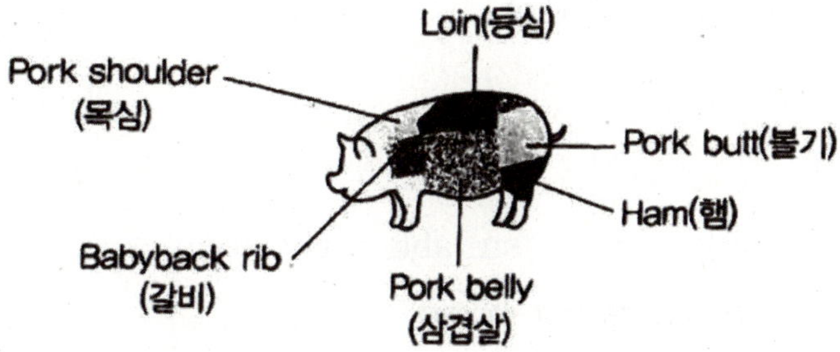

pork shoulder 목심
pork butt 볼기살
loin 등심
ham 가공한 뒷 넓적다리 부위

bacon 소금 훈제한 옆구리살
pork belly 뱃살(삼겹살 부위)
spare ribs 갈비
babyback rib 갈비

Review & Exercises

1. Words to memorize in this unit

overdone 너무 익힌
tough 질긴
apologize 사과하다
awfully 매우, 몹시
favor 호의(를 베풀다)
sodium 염분

2. Key expressions to memorize in this unit

1. This is not what I ordered.
2. Would you like something else while you are waiting?
3. I'm afraid the orders got mixed up.
4. Is everything all right, sir?
5. Would you like it cooked a little more?
6. I haven't been served yet.
7. I'm sorry to have kept you waiting, sir.
8. Would you exchange it for me?
9. Will you do me a favor?
10. I'm on a low sodium diet.

3. Exercises

1) Fill in the blank with the suitable preposition.

a. I'm afraid the orders got mixed ______.
b. I didn't know salmon is ______ the entrée.
c. Can I have chicken instead ______ fish.
d. I'm ______ a low sodium diet.

2) Pair Activity

다음 대화에서 웨이터 부분을 주어진 단어를 사용하여 완성하고 파트너와 연습하세요.

W : (Order)

G : Well, I'm not quite sure what to have.

W : (The veal?)

G : All right. I'll have that.

W : (To start?)

G : Almond soup, please.

W : (Wine?)

G : Yes. A bottle of house white, please.

Restaurant Quiz

1. Which of the following wines should be served chilled? (있는대로 선택)

   a) Red wine　　b) White wine

   c) Champagne　　d) Rose

2. When serving wine around a table, what direction should you move in?

   a) Clockwise from the host's left

   b) Counter-clockwise from the host's right

나는
레스토랑 영어다

Paying the Bill & Goodbye

Unit 9

Paying the Bill & Goodbye

Unit 9

Paying the Bill & Goodbye

Preview : Reading

▣ Western Table Manners(서양 식사 예절)

1) You should wait at the entrance of the restaurant until the waiter or waitress comes to guide you to your seat. Do not go straight to the table by yourself. In case of fast food restaurants, you may go straight to any seat.

2) When you're sitting at a table, sit up straight and comfortably. Do not rest your elbows on the table.

3) Do not tuck in or tie your napkin around your neck. The napkin belongs on your lap.

4) Use the outside fork and knife first. The Europeans hold the knife in their right hand, and the fork in their left, while the Americans change the fork from the left to the right hand after cutting their food. Never eat with your knife.

5) Eat soup as quickly as possible, with no sucking noises; this applies to coffee or tea, too.

6) While you are eating, do not bend forward with your face to the food. Food should be brought to the mouth. You can have a conversation, however, do not speak with your mouth full.

7) In case you have to leave the table during your meal, put your napkin on the armrest or on the back of the chair. Otherwise, the waiter or waitress will take your dish away.

8) Do not belch. (In Western countries, however, blowing your nose at the table is not considered rude.)

▣ Key Words

elbow	팔꿈치	sucking	홀짝이는, 빨아먹는
tuck in	쑤셔 넣다	belch	트림하다
lap	무릎	armrest	팔걸이

▣ Reading Helper

1. 안내받기 전에 입구에 기다릴 것
2. 좌석에서는 반듯하고 편안하게 앉기, 팔꿈치 괴지 않기
3. 냅킨은 무릎에
4. 나이프와 포크는 바깥쪽 것부터 사용
5. 수프, 커피 등은 소리 안내고 마시기
6. 먹을 때 고개를 너무 숙이지 않고, 입에 음식 넣은 채 말하지 않기

7. 식사 중 자리를 뜰 때 냅킨 위치에 주의

8. 트림하지 말 것

Basic Vocabulary

▣ Fill in the blank with the meaning in Korean.

split	all together
treat	receipt
absolutely	change
Dutch	policy
separate	pride

Key Expressions

▣ Make a full sentence using the words given in the bracket.

1. 계산서를 받을 수 있을까요?
(the check, I, can, please, have, ?)

____

2. 이것은 분명히 제가 냅니다.
(my, is, this, insist, I, treat)

____

3. 우리 각자 냅시다.
(Dutch, go, let's)

4. 식사가 즐거웠기를 바랍니다.
(hope, enjoyed, meal, your, you, I)

5. 어떤 방식으로 지불하시겠습니까 선생님?
(How, pay, to, like, would, you, sir,?)

6. 마스터 카드를 받아주십니까?
(Master card, do, accept, you, ?)

7. 개별적 계산서 아니면 한꺼번에 하는 것, 어느 쪽을 선호하세요?
(which, all together, or, prefer, to separate bill, you, would, have it, ?)

8. 여기에 서명 좀 해 주시겠어요?
(could, here, sign, you, please, ?)

9. 거스름돈은 당신이 가지셔도 됩니다.
(You, change, keep, can, the)

10. 팁 안 받는 것이 우리의 방침입니다.
(our, tipping, no, policy, is)

Dialogues

Dialogue 1

W : Waitress G : Guest

G1 Waitress! Can I have the check, please?

W Yes, sir I'll be along in a moment. Here you are, sir.

G2 Let's split the bill, Daniel. What do I owe you?

G1 Absolutely not! This is my treat, I insist.

Notes

♠ split 쪼개다
♠ owe 빚지다
♠ What do I owe you? =How much do I owe you? 얼마 드리면 되지요?
♠ Absolutely not! 절대로 안됩니다.
♠ This is my treat 이건 내가 낼게요.

Dialogue 2

W : Waiter G : Guest

W Would you like anything else?

G1 No, thank you. Can I have the check, please?

W Sure. There you go.

G2 Please, Paul. I'll get this.

G1 No way!

G2 Let's go Dutch, then?

Notes

♠ Can I have the check, please? 계산서 좀 받을 수 있습니까?

♠ I'll get this. = This is my treat 제가 내겠습니다.

♠ Let's go Dutch. 우리 각자 냅시다.

Dialogue 3

W : Waiter G : Guest C : Cashier

G Can I have the bill?

W Yes, ma'am. Here is your bill.

G Where is the cashier's desk?

W Right over there, ma'am.

(a little later)

C Good evening, ma'am.

G Hi! Can you charge it to my room account? I'm in 506.

C Certainly, ma'am. Room 506. Just a moment, please. That's Ms. Kim?

G Yes, that's right.

C Thank you. I hope you enjoyed your meal. Have a pleasant evening.

Notes

♠ Can you charge it to my room account? 제 방 값에 포함해 주시겠어요?

♠ I hope you enjoyed your meal. 즐거운 식사였기를 바랍니다.

Dialogue 4

C : Cashier G : Guest

C Did you enjoy your meal?

G Yes, I did. It was really delicious.

C How would you like to pay, sir?

G Do you accept Master card?

C Certainly, sir. Which would you prefer, to separate bill or have it all together?

G All together, please.

C Here's the total amount, sir. Could you sign here, please?

G OK.

(after signing)

C Thank you, sir. Here is your receipt. We hope you enjoyed your meal. Hope to see you again.

Notes

- ♠ Did you enjoy your meal? 계산하려고 하는 손님에게 Cashier가 반드시 먼저 해야 할 표현
- ♠ How would you like to pay, sir? 어떻게 지불하시겠어요?
- ♠ Do you accept Master card? 마스터카드 받으십니까?
- ♠ Which would you prefer, separate bill or to have it all together? 계산서를 따로 해 드릴까요 하나로 해 드릴까요?
- ♠ separate 분리된
- ♠ all together 한꺼번에 처리하는
- ♠ receipt 영수증 / risi:t / 발음에 유의

Dialogue 5

C : Cashier G : Guest

C Did you enjoy your meal, sir?

G Very good. I'll pay my bill now. How much is it?

C Wait a minute, please. It'll be 85,000 won altogether, sir.

G What's this total for?

C Your bill **includes** a 10% tax and a 10% **service charge.**

G I see.

C How would you like to pay, sir?

G In cash, please.

C Thank you sir. You gave me 100,000 won, Your change is 15,000 won and here is your receipt.

G **You can keep the change.**

C No, thank you, sir. **No tipping is our policy.** Have a nice day.

Notes

♠ includes 포함하다

♠ service charge 봉사료

♠ You can keep the change. 잔돈은 가지세요.

♠ No tipping is our policy. 팁 안 받는 것이 우리의 방침입니다.
= No tipping is our pride. 팁 안 받는 것이 우리의 자랑입니다.

Grammar

▣ Too + 형용사

불평을 말할 때는 'too + 형용사' 표현을 많이 쓴다. 또한 예상하고 기대했던 만큼 이루어지지 않았음을 뜻할 때에 쓰는 표현인 'It is expected to be ~' 혹은 'It is supposed to be ~'로 문장을 시작하여 아쉬움을 표시한다.

> Oh, my steak is too rare. It's expected to be medium.
> My mushroom soup is too cold. It's supposed to be warm.

위 예문들처럼 다음 문장들을 완성시켜 보시오.

1 rare / medium It's too rare. It's expected to be medium.
2 tough / tender ______________________________.
3 thick / thin ______________________________.
4 noisy / quiet ______________________________.
5 spicy / mild ______________________________.

Restaurant English Tips

▣ Regions of the U.S.A.

미국 대륙에는 time zone이 4개가 있다. 그러니까 서부 해안의 Pacific Standard Time과 동부 해안의 Eastern Standard Time은 3시간 차이다. 미국에서는 4월 마지막 일요일부터 10월 마지막 일요일까지 실시되는 Eastern Daylight

Savings Time이라는 것이 있는데, 4월 마지막 일요일에 시계를 1시간 빨리 해 놓고 가을에, 즉 10월 마지막 일요일에 다시 1시간을 늦춰 놓는다. 한국은 뉴욕보다 14시간이 빠르고 (Daylight Savings 때는 13시간), 캘리포니아보다는 11시간 빠르다. (Daylight Savings 때는 10시간). 미국을 우리는 the U.S.A.라고 하지만 실제로 보통 많이 쓰는 말은 the U.S. 아니면 the States라고 한다.

Pacific Standard Time (태평양 표준시)
Mountain Standard Time (산악 표준시)
Central Standard Time (중부 표준시)
Eastern Standard Time (동부 표준시)

미국인들은 보통 New York을 'Big Apple'이라고 부른다. 모든 사람들에게 주어지는 기회를 사과로 비유하여 누구에게나 성공의 기회가 주어진다는 뜻에서 그렇게 부른다. 오래 전에는 미국을 'melting pot'라고도 했다. 냄비에서 녹듯이 잘 섞인다는 뜻. 요즘은 그 말이 'salad bowl'로 바뀌었다. 샐러드 그릇에 담긴 여러 야채들처럼 자신들의 개성을 살리면서도 한편으로는 여러 민족이 함께 어울려 독특한 맛을 낸다는 뜻이다.

Review & Exercises

1. Words to memorize in this unit

split 쪼개다
treat 대접하다
absolutely 절대적으로
Dutch 네덜란드식의
separate 분리된
all together 한꺼번에
receipt 영수증
change 거스름돈
policy 정책, 방침
pride 자긍심

2. Key expressions to memorize in this unit

1. Can I have the check, please?
2. This is my treat, I insist.
3. Let's go Dutch.
4. I hope you enjoyed your meal.
5. How would you like to pay, sir?
6. Do you accept Master card?
7. Which would you prefer, to separate bill or have it all together?
8. Could you sign here, please?
9. You can keep the change.
10. No tipping is our policy.

3. Exercises

1) Fill in the blank with the suitable word.

a. Let's _______ Dutch, then?

b. Which would you prefer, to separate bill or have it all _______?

c. You can _______ the change.

d. No _______ is our policy

2) Fill in the blank and practice with your partner.

W : Waiter G : Guest

W : Would you like anything else?

G1 : No, thank you. Can I _______________, please?
(계산서 좀 주시겠어요)

W : Sure. There you go.

G2 : Please, Paul. I'll ___________________.
(이건 제가 내겠습니다)

G1 : No way!

G2 : ____________________, then?

(그럼 우리 각자 냅시다)

Restaurant Quiz

1. How do you prevent dripping when you finish pouring wine?

   a) Twist the bottle as you bring it up.
   b) You can't.

2. How much wine should you pour into each guest's glass?

   a) Fill the glass b) Two-thirds of a glass
   c) Half a glass

Room Services

Unit **10**

Room Services

Unit 10

Room Services

식당을 열기 전이나 닫은 후에 식사를 주문하고 싶으면 room service를 이용하면 된다. 호텔에는 대체로 24시간의 룸서비스가 있으며 심야메뉴도 풍부하다. 외국의 호텔에 묵었는데 시차로 잠이 안 와서 뭔가 먹고 싶어졌을 때 이용하면 편리하다. 룸서비스를 주문하려면 직접 방에서 전화하던가 호텔의 operator를 통해서 룸서비스에게 연결해 달라던가 하면 된다. 또 식사를 가져온 호텔 종업원에게는 약간의 tip을 주는 관례이다. 아침식사 room service의 경우, 방에 비치된 주문서를 기재하여 그것을 방의 door handle에 걸어두면 되는 호텔도 요즈음엔 많이 있다.

Preview : Reading

▣ Room Service

Room service is one of the most important service functions at a hotel. Very often, guests call the room service and give them orders.

1. Room Service is a food delivery system. The right food should be delivered in the right room at the right time.

2. The key people in room service are the order taker, the waiter, and the cook. The order taker writes the guest's order accurately.
3. The waiter sees that the guest's wishes are carried out.
4. The cook cooperates with the waiter by preparing the food on time.

▣ Key Words

function	기능	see(to it) that ~	~에 주의하다
delivery	배달	carry out	수행하다
accurately	정확하게	cooperate	협동하다

▣ Reading Helper

1 호텔에서 가장 중요한 서비스 기능 중 하나
2 식음료배달시스템 / 올바른 음식, 올바른 시간, 올바른 객실
3 룸서비스 구성 요원 : Order-taker, Waiter, Cook

Basic Vocabulary

▣ Fill in the blank with the meaning in Korean.

room service	champagne
order	soft boiled
a bottle of beer	hard boiled
desk drawer	sunny-side up
forgive the delay	clam chowder

Key Expressions

▣ Make a full sentence using the words given in the bracket.

1. 대륙식 조찬 2인분을 예약하고자 합니다.
(we, have, breakfast, two, for, a continental, to, want)

2. 커피 혹은 티를 드시겠어요?
(coffee or tea, you, would, for, care, ?)

3. 성함과 객실 번호를 말씀해 주세요.
(name, please, room number, have, I, may, your, and, ?)

4. 즉시 가져다 드리겠습니다.
(I'll, immediately, have, to you, it, sent)

5. 지연됨에 대해서 용서해주세요.
(delay, forgive, the, please)

6. 저녁 식사 2인분을 예약하고 싶습니다.
(I'd, two, reserve, to, supper, like, for)

7. 어떤 종류의 메뉴가 있으세요?
(what, menu, you, kind, do, have, of, ?)

8. 책상 서랍 안에 메뉴를 발견하실 수 있을 것입니다 손님.
(You'll, desk drawer, a menu, the, in, find, sir)

9. 샴페인을 약간 주문하려고 합니다.
(I'd, champagne, order, to, like, some)

10. 몇 시에 서비스받기를 원하세요?
(What time, it, like, served, you, would, sir, ?)

Dialogues

Dialogue 1

R : Room Service G : Guest

R Good morning, Room Service, may I help you?
G Hello, **we want to have a continental breakfast for two.**
R Very well, sir. Which juice would you like, tomato or orange?
G One orange and one tomato.
R All right, sir. Would you **care for** coffee or tea?
G Bring us coffee, please.

R Very well, sir. May I have your name and room number, please?

G This is Mr. Brown in room 1117.

Notes

♠ We want to have a continental breakfast for two. 대륙식 조찬 2인분 부탁합니다.

♠ care for = like

♠ May I have your name and room number, please? 성함과 방번호가 어떻게 되십니까?

Dialogue 2

R : Room Service G : Guest

R Good afternoon, Room Service, may I help you?

G Hello, this is Mr. Chung in room 1234. I would like to order some spaghetti with meat sauce.

R Yes, sir. Anything else?

G Do you have clam chowder?

R Yes, we do.

G Okay, bring me some clam chowder and coffee, please.

Notes

♠ clam chowder 대합 조개로 만든 차우더

Dialogue 3

R : Room Service Clerk G : Guest

R Room service, Miss Kim speaking. May I help you?

G Yes, this is Mr. Banning in 209. I ordered a bottle of beer about 20 minutes ago, but you still haven't sent it.

R I'm terribly sorry, Mr. Banning. I'll have it sent to you immediately. Please forgive the delay.

G That's alright. Thank you.

Notes

♠ have it sent (사역동사 have + 목적어 + 과거분사) : 올려 보내겠습니다.
♠ immediately (=at once) : 즉시
♠ forgive the delay : 늦어진 것에 대해 용서해 주세요.

Dialogue 4

R : Room Service Clerk G : Guest

R Good evening. May I help you, sir?

G Yes, please. I'd like to reserve supper for two.

R Very well, sir. May I take your order now?

G What kind of menu do you have?

R You'll find a menu in the desk drawer, sir.

G Oh, really? Wait a moment, please. I've found the menu. Let me see... Please bring me tomato juice, two eggs sunny-side up, buttered toast and coffee.

R What time would you like it served, sir?

G At 7:30.

R Yes, sir. May I have your name and room number, please?

G My name is Green. Room number's 1237.

R Thank you for calling, sir.

Notes

- ♠ supper for two (persons) : 2인분 저녁 식사
- ♠ What kind of menu do you have? 어떤 메뉴를 갖고 계세요?
- ♠ take your order : 주문을 받다
- ♠ You'll find a menu in the desk drawer, sir. 책상 서랍 속에 메뉴가 있을 겁니다
- ♠ sunny-side up : 계란의 한쪽 흰자만 익힌 것
- ♠ buttered toast : 버터 바른 토스트 빵
- ♠ What time would you like it served, sir? 몇 시에 서비스 받기를 원하세요?

Dialogue 5

R : Room Service Clerk G : Guest

R Room service. May I help you, sir?

G Yes, I'd like to order **some champagne.**

R How many bottles, sir?

G Two, please. And **make sure** they're cold.

R Certainly, sir. May I have your name and room number, please?

G Smith. Room 1234.

Notes

♠ some champagne : 약간의 샴페인 (champagne 셀 수 없는 명사)

c.f. two bottles of champagne : 샴페인 두 병 (bottle 셀 수 있는 명사)

♠ make sure (that) S + V : 확실하게 하다

Grammar

▣ What ~ like? 구문

> **How** is the soup?
>
> ➡ **What** is the soup **like?** (수프가 어떻습니까?)

"What ~ like"는 "How"와 같은 뜻이다. 위 예문처럼 '?는 어떤가'의 뜻이 되게 What ~~~ like? 문장을 만드시오.

1) How is the weather?

➡ ____?

2) How is the restaurant?

➡ ____?

3) How is the local beer?

➡ ____?

4) How is the beaches?

➡ ____?

5) How is the music?

➡ ____?

6) How is the facilities?

➡ ____?

Restaurant English Tips

▣ British and American English

British English	American English	Meaning
accommodation	accommodations	숙박시설
alter	change	변경하다
aubergine	eggplant	가지

barman	bartender	바텐더
bill (for food)	check	계산서
biscuit	cookie	쿠키
cheque	check	수표
colour	color	색깔
courgette	zucchini	호박
cupboard, wardrobe	closet	찬장, 벽장
curtains	drapes	커튼
enquiry	inquiry	문의
fill in	fill out	(양식에) 기입해넣다
form	blank/form	양식, 형식
fridge	icebox	냉동고
hairdrier	hair dryer	헤어드라이어
holiday	vacation	휴가
interconnecting	adjoining	인접한
labour	labor	노동
lager	beer	맥주
licence	license	면허
lift	elevator	승강기
luggage	baggage/luggage	수하물
main course	entrée	주요리
note (paper money)	bill	지폐
page boy	bell boy, bell hop	벨맨
post	mail	우편
provisional	unconfirmed	임시의
pub	saloon/bar	술집
purse	pocket book	지갑
reception	front desk/front office	안내데스크
receptionist	clerk, desk clerk	안내직원
rubbish	garbage/trash	쓰레기
shop	store	상점
spirit	liquor	술
starter	appetizer	식전요리

sunglasses	shades	색안경
syndicate room	conference room	회의실
tap	faucet	수도꼭지
taxi	cab	택시
toilet	bathroom/restroom/washroom	화장실
traveller's cheques	travelers checks	여행자수표
waiter	waiter/food server	웨이터
washbasin	sink	씽크대

Review & Exercises

1. Words to memorize in this unit

room service 룸서비스

order 주문하다

a bottle of beer 맥주 한 병

desk drawer 책상 서랍

sunny-side up 한 면만 프라이한 계란

clam chowder 대합조개 차우더

forgive the delay 지연됨을 용서하다

champagne 샴페인

soft boiled 반숙계란

hard boiled 완숙계란

2. Key expressions to memorize in this unit

1. We want to have a continental breakfast for two.
2. Would you care for coffee or tea?
3. May I have your name and room number, please?
4. I'll have it sent to you immediately.
5. Please forgive the delay.
6. I'd like to reserve supper for two.
7. What kind of menu do you have?

8. You'll find a menu in the desk drawer, sir.
9. I'd like to order some champagne.
10. What time would you like it served?

3. Exercises

1) Fill in the blank with the suitable preposition.

a. Would you care ______ coffee or tea?

b. I'd like to reserve supper ______ two.

2) Pair Activity : Room Service Substitution Drill

보기에 주어진 정보를 넣어서 파트너와 다음 대화를 연습하세요.

A : Good evening, this is Room Service. How may I help you?

B : Hi, this is Mr. Smith in room 911. Is it possible to get __________ delivered to my room?

A : Yes, please go ahead and make your order.

B : Well, I'd like to have ______________.

A : Would you care to have anything else?

B : Hmmm... I'd also like ______________, please.

A : We'll bring your meal to you as soon as possible.

Type of Order Wanted	First Order	Second Order
breakfast	some bacon and toast	a glass of orange juice
lunch	a club sandwich	some potato chips
dinner	the fried chicken dinner	some egg rolls
a snack	some assorted nuts	a fruit platter

3) Put the following into English.

1) 지금 주문하시겠어요?

____?

2) 어떤 메뉴가 있습니까?

____?

3) 2인용 저녁 식사를 예약하고 싶습니다

____?

4) 몇 시에 갖다 드리기를 원하십니까?

____?

5) 전화 주셔서 감사합니다.

____.

4) Complete the dialogue.

C : Clerk G : Guest

C : Room service. ______________________________, sir.
1) (무엇을 도와 드릴까요?)

G : Yes. ____.
2) (샴페인을 약간 주문하고자 합니다)

C : ______________________________, sir?
3) (몇 병이나 드릴까요?)

G : Two, please. And ______________________ they're cold.
4) (확실히 차갑게 해 주세요)

C : Certainly, sir. ____?

5) (성함과 객실 번호가 어떻게 되십니까?)

G : Smith. Room 1234.

Restaurant Quiz

1. When do you think is the busiest time for room service?

   a) It's at breakfast time. b) It's at lunch time.
   c) It's at dinner time.

2. It is unnecessary for the room-service waiter to know the proper way to serve wine.

   a) True b) False

All-in-One Restaurant Service

Unit 11

All-in-One Restaurant Service

레스토랑 서비스영어 종합편

Unit 10

All-in-One Restaurant Service

레스토랑 서비스영어 종합편

1. 입구에서 손님 맞이하기

"Good (Time of day Sir/Madam(name of the guest)!"

"Welcome to Morning Star(Name of Restaurant)."

e.g. "Good morning, sir/ma'am! Welcome to Morning Star."

2. 손님이 예약을 하였는지 문의

"Do you have a reservation with us, sir/madam?"

"Have you made a reservation?"

"May I ask if you have made a reservation?"

예약을 했다고 하면..

"May I have you name, sir/madam?"

만약 이름을 찾을 수 없다면..

"Mr/Mrs... Could it be under any other name besides...?
(혹 다른 분 성함으로 예약하신 건 아니신지요?)

만약 이름을 찾았다면..

"(Name of guest) You have reserved a table for (number of people) by the ...
Is that correct? We have a tabler ready/waiting for you."

e.g. Mr. Kim. You have reserved a table for 4 people by the window. Is that correct? We have a table ready/waiting for you.

만약 손님이 예약을 하지 않았다면...

"May I know how many are in your party?"

"May I have your name for our reference?"

"Is there any preference in seating?"
e.g. by the window OR booth table OR by the kitchen view

"(Name of the guest) The waiting time would be approximately ... minutes .... Is it alright with you?"

"While we have your table ready, would you like to have a glass of cocktail/wine at the bar? We will inform you as soon as your table is ready."

3. 코트, 큰가방, 우산 등을 들어드리고자 제안할 때

"(Name of the guest), May I assist you with your coat/bag/umbrella?"

"Do you any valuable items in your bag/coat? Would you please have them with you?"

4. 손님을 안내할 때

"(Name of the guest), Please come this way."

"Please let me escort to your table."

"May I know if this is your first visit to Morning Star(Name of Restaurant)?

"Please watch your steps ahead."

5. 손님을 자리에 앉히기

"(Name of the guest). Will this be fine?"

"Please take a seat."

6. 메뉴 보여주기(음료와 음식)

"Excuse me (Name of the guest). These are our menus. You see are the wine, á la carte, set menu and promotion menus."

"My colleague (name of the colleague) will be with you shortly. Enjoy your breakfast/lunch/dinner."

7. 손님의 이름을 팀 리더나 웨이터에게 알려주기

8. 웨이터 혹은 팀 리더의 인사

"Good (time of the day). Mr/Mrs/Ms..... How are you?"

"How are you doing this afternoon/evening?"

9. 냅킨 펼쳐주기

"Excuse me..."

10. 빵과 무료로 제공되는 전채요리 서비스

"Excuse me... this is our bread and a dip with complimentary welcome appetizer ..... Enjoy."

11. 제 1 단계 음료 요청(Ask for 1st round drinks)

"May I recommend a glass of (name of the drink) to start?"

"Thank you. I will be right back with your (name of the drink.)"

12. 주문 넣기

13. 바에서 주문한 것 가져오기

14. 제 1단계 음료 서빙하기

"(Name of the guest). Here is your (Name of the cocktail)."

"Enjoy your (name of the drink)"

15. á la carte(일품요리) 주문 요청하기

"(Name of the guest). Have you decided on what you would like?"

"Would you like to order?"

"May I take your order?"

주문이 주어지는 동안에 손님들에게 주어진 주문을 확인할 때 하면 좋은 표현들

"That is an excellent choice!"

"How did you know it is the most popular items?"

"You are going to love your breakfast/lunch/dinner."

업셀링(unselling)을 위해 추천되는 표현들

"May I recommend the (구체적인 요리이름) to start!"

"The Chef prepares an excellent (구체적인 요리)! Would you like to try?"

"(Name of the dish) is most popular dish from our menu, would you like to try?"

주문을 반복하기

"(Name of the guest). Please allow me to repeat your order. For appetizer, you've ordered ..... and ..... Followed by ..... and ..... as main course. Is that correct?

16. 주문 넣기

17. 주문에 따라서 테이블을 세팅하기

18. 첫 번째 주문(appetizer)을 키친에서 가져오기

19. 애프타이저를 서빙하기

"(Name of the guest). Here is your delicious (name of the dish)."

"The plate is hot. Please be careful."

"Bon appetite/Enjoy your (name of the dish)."

20. 테이블의 상황을 체크하고 손님에게 끊임없이 바디랭귀지로 대화하기

21. 손님의 만족도를 체크하기!

음식에 대한 체크

"How is your (name of the dish)?"

"Are you enjoying (name of the dish)?"

"How are you with your (name of the dish)?"

테이블의 분위기 유지하기

"May I refresh your drink?"

"May I refresh your bread/olive oil?"

"May I pour you more wine?"

"Is there anything I can get you at this time?"

22. 애프타이저 접시 치우기

"Are you through with your (name of the dish)?"

"May I clear your plates?"

23. 테이블 정리하기

24. 메인 코스 준비하기

25. 메인 코스 서빙하기

"(Name of the guest). Here is your delicious (name of the dish)"

"The plate is hot. Plerase be careful."

"Bon appetite/Enjoy your (name of the dish)."

26. 테이블의 상황을 체크하고 손님에게 끊임없이 바디랭귀지로 대화하기

27. 손님의 만족도를 체크하기!!

음식에 대한 체크

"How is your (name of the dish)?"

"Are you enjoying (name of the dish)?"

"How are you with your (name of the dish)?"

테이블의 분위기 유지

"May I refresh your drink?"

"May I refresh your bread/olive oil?"

"May I pour you more wine?"

"Is there anything I can get you at this time?"

28. 메인 코스 치우기

"Are you through with your (name of the dish)?"

"May I clear your plates?"

"We have lovely dessert waiting for you. Would you like to look at our menu?"

29. 디저트 주문 들어가기

"May I take your dessert order?"

"Have you decided on what you would like?"

업셀링 표현들

"A cup of coffee/tea would be great with your (name of the dish). Would you like to have one?"

"How about a cup of coffee/tea with your (name of the dessert)?"

"May be a glass of port or dessert wine?"

30. 디저트 서빙하기

"Here is the best (name of the dessert) in town."

"Here is your (name of the dessert)."

"Enjoy your (name of the dessert)."

31. 손님의 계산서 준비하기

"Yes (name of the dish). I will be right back with your bill."

32. 계산서를 손님에게 드리기

"Excuse me. (name of the guest). Here is your bill. Mr... do you havea valet ticket with you?"

손님이 현금으로 지불한다면...

"Thank you very much! I will be right back with your change."

손님이 호텔방 요금에 포함시키고자 한다면...

"Please print your name, your room number and we4 would also require your signature!"

"Thank you very much."

손님이 신용카드로 지불하고자 한다면...

"Thank you very much! I will be right back."

"(name of the guest). We require your signature on the credit receipt."

"May I have your signature please?"

"You will find the receipt in the envelope."

"Thank you very much."

33. 손님을 출구까지 에스코트하고 작별인사 하기

"Have you enjoyed your dinner at Morning Star(name of the restaurant)?"

"We hope to see you soon."

"We hope to see you in the near future."

"Thank you for dining with us. Please enjoy rest of your evening."

34. 손님에게 코트, 큰 가방, 우산 등을 챙겨주기

"(name of the guest). May I please have your coat tag? Thank you."

"How was your overall experience at Morning Star(name of the restaurant)?"

"Would you like to make reservations for another occasions?"

"Thank you very much. Have a pleasant afternoon/evening."

Activity 1 : Word Study (the top 10 useful words)

레스토랑 서비스에서 가장 빈도수가 높은 단어들로 구성된 보기에서 단어들을 골라 10개의 중요한 구문을 완성하시오.

pay, compliment, kitchen, receipt, bill, meal, accept, chef, rare, mistake

1. The ____________ prepared meals for the restaurant's guests all day long.
2. Mr. Kim gave a ____________ to the waitress for her excellent service.
3. Here is the ____________ and your credit card.
4. I must have made a ____________ and charged you for the wrong meal.
5. She's going to ____________ for her meal with cash.

6. Could you give me the ____________ as soon as possible?
7. This is the best ____________ I've ever eaten at this restaurant.
8. Would you like your steak cooked ____________, medium, or well done?
9. I'll go back to the ____________ and check on your meal.
10. I'm sorry, but we don't ____________ personal checks.

Activity 2 : Match the related sentences.

1. Shall I bring you a drink? ( )
2. Is everything all right? ( )
3. Did you enjoy your meal tonight? ( )
4. Can I interest you in some dessert? ( )
5. I have a reservation for 8:00 tonight? ( )
6. How would you like to pay? ( )
7. It's the chef's own special recipe. ( )

a) It sounds wonderful.
b) May I please have your name?
c) Well, I've already eaten a lot.
d) Actually, I'm afraid there is a small problem.
e) You accept credit cards, don't you?
f) Yes, I'd like to have a glass of the house wine.
g) It was one of the best meals I've had in a long time.

Activity 3 : Mixed-up Order Taking

다음 네 사람이 아침 식사를 주문했는데 그들의 주문 사항이 엉켜버렸다. 누가 무엇을 주문했는지 알아내시오. 각 사람은 세 개의 음식 적어도 음료수 하나는 주문했다.

	Drinks		Food items		
	Juice	Hot drink	1	2	3
Jeff					
Pierre					
Susanna					
Helen					

a. Jeff has ordered orange juice and coffee.

b. Helen wants croissants.

c. Everyone wants orange juice except one person, who wants grapefruit juice and tea.

d. Every wants either eggs or croissants, but nobody wants both.

e. One man and one woman have ordered eggs.

f. The woman who wants fried eggs wants orange juice and no hot drink.

g. The man who is having coffee does not want croissants.

h. The man who wants croissants also wants orange juice and hot chocolate.

I. Both croissant-eaters want butter, but only the woman wants jam.

j. The person with no hot drink has ordered sausages and mushrooms.

k. The person who wants fruit yoghurt does not drink coffee.

l. The person who wants scrambled eggs has also ordered toast and butter.

나는 레스토랑 영어다

Appendix

1. English Interview
2. 유명인사들의 좌우명
3. An Interview Model for a Hotel Clerk
4. Food & Beverage Terms

1 English Interview(영어면접)

■ English Interview for getting a Job

예시 자기소개 Let Me Introduce Myself

Hi, everyone. It's nice to meet you all. Let me briefly introduce myself. My name is Young-hee Lee. I live in Seoul, but I'm originally from Anyang. I am a student at Daelim University College and my major is hotel and Food and Beverage Service. I also work part time at a coffee shop. so I'm pretty busy and tired. However, I work hard because I want to become an able hotelier in the future.

◉ 영어면접의 종류 (Types of English Interview)

1. Interview with Korean interviewer (내국인 영어면접)
2. Interview with native speakers (외국인 영어면접)
3. Personal interview (개별 면접)
4. Group interview (그룹 면접)
5. Team assessment (팀 평가 면접)
6. Group discussion (그룹 토론)
7. Role play (역할극)

◉ 어떻게 준비하나 (How to Prepare)

1. Research applying airlines
2. Be familiar with aviation knowledge
3. Know yourself.
4. Practice makes perfect.
5. Study with peers.
6. Practice answering a lot of different questions naturally.

◉ Interview Day Tips (면접당일 면접의 팁)

1. Be honest and open.
2. Be positive and show your interest.
3. Keep your sense of humor and show your smile consistently.
4. Don't prepare a long speech.
5. Don't be nervous.
6. Prepare your own questions about the company.

▣ 면접의 일반적 상황 (Situations)

예시 인사

A : Interviewee(면접당사자) B : Interviewer(면접관)

A : Good morning, sir.

B : Good morning. It's god to meet you. Please have a seat and make yourself comfortable.

A : Thank you, sir.

B : How are you doing?

A : I am fine, thank you. How are you?

B : I am also fine, thank you.

예시 인사 후 예상 질문

1. 간단한 자기 소개

이름, 출신, 가족, 학력, 군복무, 취미, 개인이 추구하는 목표 등

B : Let's get started. Please tell me a little bit about yourself.

A : My name is Soo-Hee Lee. Lee is my family name. I am 25 years old. I was born and raised in Pusan, the south part of Korea. I have five members in my family - my parents, one elder brother and one younger sister.

I graduated from ____ High School in 1996. I served in the army from 2010 to 2012. I have been studying hotel management for two years at __________College.

My favorite hobbies are mountain climbing, fishing, and studyng English. My personal goal is to be the best hotel manager in Korea.

2. 원하는 직종

B : Thank you very much. I notice you speak very good English.

A : Oh, do I? Thank you, sir. English has always fascinated me, and I realize that it is very important to know.

B : That's right. It's especially important for someone who will work with foreigners, such as a hotel personnel. What job are you applying for?

A : I would like to start out as a waiter, but I would be willing to work at any job to gain hotel experience.

3. 관련 직종에서의 경험 유무

B : Well, with your English language ability, you would be a good candidate for a waiter. Have you ever worked in a restaurant before?

A : No, I haven't. However, I am finishing my education at ________ College, majoring in hotel management.

B : That's a very wonderful school, I know.

4. 자신의 장점 및 고객과 문제 발생시 대처 방법

B : What do you think is your best characteristic?

A : I am a "can-do" person. When I am given a job, I do it. I don't like to leave any task unfinished.

B : That's very admirable. Let me give you a situation. If you were a waiter and a guest had some problem, what would you do?

A : First, I would find out what the problem is. If it is something I can handle, I will take care of it immediately. In any case, I would like to make sure that the guest is satisfied.

▣ More on Expressions of English Interview

(1) 인사하기

Questions	Possible Answers
- How are you? - How are you doing? - How are you feeling today? - How are things going?	- I'm pretty good, thank you. - I'm fine but a little nervous. - I'm pleased to be here.

첫 인상의 중요성. 면접관과 눈이 마주치면 당황하지 말고 긴장을 풀고 자신감 있게 인사하자.

(2) 소개하기

– Please introduce yourself. – Tell me about yourself. – Would you like to introduce yourself?	– Certainly, sir. I am Lee Suyoung who is applying for a hotelier position. I am majoring in Hotel Management & Food and Beverage Service at ________________.

(3) 개인 신상에 관한 질문

1) 가족관계 (Family)

– How many people are there in your family? Can you tell me about your family?	– There are five of us in my family. My parents, an elder sister, a younger brother and me. – My father is an accountant, and my mother is a teacher.... my brother is serving army.

저희는 대가족입니다.	I have a large family. I come from a big family
저는 첫째 딸입니다.	I am the oldest(=eldest) daughter.
저는 외동입니다.	I am the only child in my family.
저는 세 자녀 중 막내입니다.	I am the youngest of three children.
아버지를 닮았습니다.	I resemble my father.
아버지보다 어머니를 더 닮았습니다.	I take after mother more than father.
어려서 아버지가 돌아가셨습니다.	I lost my father in my childhood.

2) 신체조건 (Physical Status)

– Please tell me about your physical status: height, weight, eyesight? (당신의 신체조건, 키, 몸무게, 시력을 말씀해 주시겠습니까?)	– My height is 165 cm. I weigh 48 Kg, and my corrected eyesight is 1.0 for my right eye and 1.2 for my left eye. (키는 165 cm, 몸무게는 48 kg, 교정시력으로 오른쪽이 1.0, 왼쪽이 1.2입니다.)

3) 성격 (personality)

- What is your personality like? - What would you say about your personality? - What do you think of yourself?	- I am prudent. - I am responsible. - I like to be around people. - I consider myself flexible. - I have a sense of humor. My friends tell me that I'm funny and entertaining.

4) 장점(strength) & 단점(weakness)

- What are your strengths (weaknesses)? - What are you good at?	- I am strong-willed. I have been studying Chinese for myself during college days. Now I have not much difficulty of speaking Chinese, so I enjoyed my trip to China last summer.

5) 취미 활동(Hobbies, Personal Tastes)

- What are your hobbies? - What do you do in your free time? - What do you do for fun? - How do you spend your free time?	- I usually go to the gym for a workout. It helps me in shape, too. - I spend my free time volunteering. - I enjoy spending time with my friends in my free time. It's a great way to unwind.

취미에 대해 이야기 할 때에는 단순한 취미에 그치는 것이 아니라 취미를 통해 자기 개발에 힘쓰고 있다는 사실을 나타내도록 한다.

6) 대학 시절의 경험 관련 표현들

club activity	동아리 활동	president	회장
internship program	인턴사원 프로그램	MT(membership training)	엠티
volunteer club	봉사동아리	fund-raising	기금 모금

student representative	학생 대표	student council	학생회
a social service club	봉사동아리	broadcasting club	방송반
choir	합창단	academic fair	학술제
volunteer work	자원봉사	sports event	체육대회
photo club	사진 동아리	festival	축제
dance club	댄스 동아리	exchange program	교환학생 프로그램

(4) 업무 경험 (Job Experience)

아르바이트 등 - Did you have any part-time experience? - Did you work during college? - Tell me about your job experience	- I was an intern at Asia Hotel during summer vacation. My internship experience has prepared me to work with various people. I learned a hard lesson dealing with all sorts of people

본인이 가진 작은 경험이라도 적극적으로 알리도록 한다. 아르바이트라 할지라도 단순한 업무를 통해 긍정적 느낌이 있었거나 직업의식을 느끼는 지원자는 더 좋은 점수를 얻는다.

◉ 유용한 표현

과외(tutoring), 고객서비스(customer service), 안내(receptionist), 아기돌보기(baby-sitting), 계산원 (cashier), 서빙(serving customers)

1) 호텔에 대한 지식

- Tell me what you know about our hotel. - Do you know anything about our company? - What do you know about our company?	- Four Seasons hotel was founded in _____ and the President is _______ at the moment. Four Seasons is one of the largest hotel in Korea and is known for its high quality service. I think Four Seasons Hotel is one of the world's greatest hotels in the world.

2) 회사 지원 동기

– Why did you apply for this company? – What makes you to apply for our company?	– Your hotel is the best company in the hospitality industry. My goal is to work with the best. – I am impressed with the fact that Four Seasons Hotel has been expanding successfully. That is amazing.

회사 지원 동기를 설명할 때 그 기업의 비전 및 경영 철학, 기업 문화 등에 대해 미리 숙지하여 회사의 긍정적인 면을 부각하는 내용을 언급하라. 지원 동기는 자기소개와 더불어 면접에서 가장 많이 물어보는 내용이므로 남들이 다 같이 대답하는 평범하고 판이 박힌 내용보다는 본인의 어떤 점이 회사에 이익을 줄 수 있는지 고민하고 준비하자.

3) Hotelier라는 직업 지원 동기

– Why did you apply for this position? – Why do you want to be a flight attendant?	– It is my dream to be a hotelier since very young. It is my dream to realize my goals in your company. – I've always wanted to be a hotelier since I was a little girl. And I think working as a hotelier would give me the best opportunity to use the knowledge I've studied in college.

(5) 자신의 의견 말하기 (Personal Opinion)

1) 안전과 서비스 정신에 관하여

– Which one is more important, safety or good service?	– They are both important; however, I should put safety before good service. It is the duty of the hoteliers to ensure the customers' safety.

2) 단독 혹은 협동 작업 선호에 대해서

- Do you prefer working with others or by yourself? - Do you prefer to work individually or on a team?	- I prefer to work with others. Working in a team is more fun and better. I am certain that team players get things done faster.

3) 5년 내의 목표

- What is your goal in 5 years? - Where do you see yourself in 5 years?	- In 5 years, I can see myself as a manager at a famous hotel, I am sure that my major in college will help me perform better as a hotelier

입사 면접 단골 질문임. 5년 목표와 10년 목표로 준비

(6) Saying Goodbye (끝인사)

- Okay. That was the last question. Thank you - That's the end of the interview. We will let you know the result as soon as possible.	- Thank you, sir. I've enjoyed talking with you. - I appreciate your time, sir. I hope to see you again.

마지막 질문이 끝났다고 면접이 끝난 것 아니다. 시간을 내 준 것에 대해 감사의 인사를 전한다. 면접관에게 기억에 남을 만한 인상을 줄 수 있도록 자신이 지원하고자 하는 분야에 대한 간단한 질문을 준비하는 것도 좋다.

▣ 성공적인 영어 면접 Tip

1) 기출문제들을 연습하라 (Practice existed questions.)

한국어 질문과 달리 영어면접은 기존의 기출 문제의 범주에서 크게 벗어나지 않는다. 주로 질문하는 예상문제는 지원하는 회사에 관하여, 승무원 업무에 관련된 서비스 그리고 나머지 질문들은 본인에 관해서이다. 처음 영어면접을 준비하는 지원자들은 기출 문제로 다양한 연습을 통해서 답변을 준비하는 것이 바람직하다.

영어면접 노트를 따로 만들어서 한 페이지에 하나의 질문을 적고 답변을 적는다. 빈칸이 많이 남아도 하나씩 적으면 추후 수정할 수도 있고 그 질문에 대한 예상 꼬리 질문을 적어둘 수도 있을 것이다.

2) 자연스런 대화로 연습하라. (Converse naturally.)

처음에 영어 면접을 준비할 때는 작문한 내용을 그대로 외워서 시작하여, 완전히 자신의 영어가 되도록 연습한다. 처음에는 발음이나 억양이 부자연스러울 수 있으나 자연스런 미소를 지으며 읽고, 외울 때에도 거울을 보며 본인의 눈을 바라보며 미소 지으며 답변하는 연습을 해야 한다.

3) 간단하고 명료하게 답하라. (Make simply and clearly.)

처음 준비할 때는 열정이 과한 나머지 답변을 길게 준비하는데 아무리 좋은 답변이라도 장황한 답변은 면접관의 주의나 관심을 끌기에 부족하다. 답변은 간결하고 정확한 표현을 사용함이 중요하다. 그리고 어려운 단어보다는 본인이 발음하기 쉬운 단어로 명확하게 전달하자. 대답은 항상 결론부터 말한 뒤, 부연설명을 하도록 한다. 가장 중요한 것은 면접관과 얼마나 의사소통이 잘되는지가 면접의 포인트이다.

4) 분위기를 주도하라. (Lead!)

면접에서 지원자가 Lead를 하는 것이 가능할까? 충분히 가능하다. 처음 들어갈 때, 먼저 How are you? 라고 인사했다면 벌써 면접의 분위기를 주도한 것이다. 그리고 면접관의 질문에 답변을 할 때 머리 속에 꼬리 질문을 예상하고 답변을 한다면 면접을 이끌어 나갈 수 있을 것이며 자신감 상승의 효과와 면접관의 관심을 한 몸에 받으며 영어면접을 가뿐히 통과 할 것이다.

▣ 영어면접 시 상황에 따른 영어표현

1) 인사말은 자연스럽게

Thank you very much. 감사합니다.
Thank you for everything. 여러 가지로 감사합니다.
How kind of you to say so. 그렇게 말씀해 주시니 고맙습니다.

2) 대답은 정중하게

Yes or No 로만 대답하는 단답형을 피하고 정중한 표현으로 답변을 하도록 노력.
What would you do?라고 물을 때의 대답은 I would ~.
부정적인 답변에는 I am afraid that ~을 사용하도록 한다.

3) 질문을 알아듣지 못했을 때

다시 질문을 요청해서 정확한 답변을 하도록 하자.
확실하게 질문을 이해 못한 채 추측으로 답변하는 것은 불합격의 지름길이다.

'다시 한번 말씀해 주시겠어요?' 의 다양한 표현

I beg your pardon, sir?(ma'am)
I am afraid that I don' t quite understand. I don't catch your point.
Would you be kind of repeating for me?
Could you explain more?
Would you mind repeating it?

4) 대답하기 어려운 질문을 받았을 때

질문을 받고 무표정한 채로 가만히만 있다면 질문 자체를 이해하지 못한 것으로 오해받게 되므로 미소를 지으며 hmm... 혹은 Let me think... 혹은 Can you give me a second? 으로 답변할 시간을 요구하도록 한다. 요구한 뒤 조금의 망설임은 가능하지만 너무 간격을 두지 말도록 하자. 대답이 준비되지 않은 질문이거나 대답을 할 수 없는 경우에는 빨리 다른 기회를 정중히 요청하는 것이 옳다.

I am afraid that I don' t prepare the answer for the question correctly.
I have an idea about OOO instead of it.
If you don' t mind, could you give me another chance for me?

▣ 영어 면접 시 가훈이나 생활신조에 쓸 수 있는 표현

1. Think of today as my last day of life
   오늘을 인생의 마지막 날이라고 생각하라.
2. Treat others as you want to be treated
   네가 대접받고 싶은 만큼 남도 그렇게 대해라.
3. Time and tide wait for no men. 세월은 사람을 기다리지 않는다.
4. Honesty is the best policy. 정직이 최선의 정책이다.
5. Be generous to others but to be very strict with myself.
   타인에게는 관대하게 자신에게는 매우 엄격하게.
6. Without haste, but without rest 서둘지도 말고 그렇다고 쉬지도 말라.
7. The door of opportunity is opened by pushing.
   기회의 문은 밀어야 열린다.

8. Anything you're good at contributes to happiness.
당신이 잘하는 일이라면 무엇이나 행복에 도움이 된다.

9. A good beginning makes a good ending. 시작이 좋으면 끝도 좋다.

10. Step by step one goes a long way. 천리 길도 한 걸음부터

11. All in good time. 모든 일에는 때가 있는 법이다.

12. Better the last smile than the first laughter. 진정한 승자는 나중에 웃는다.

13. If you laugh, blessing will come your way. 웃으면 복이 와요.

14. When the word is out, it belongs to another. 한번 뱉은 말은 되돌릴 수 없다.

2 유명인사들의 좌우명

이름	직업 또는 직책	좌우명 (한글)	좌우명 (영어)
크리스 올브렉트 조지 스타인브레너	홈박스 오피스 CEO 뉴욕 양키스 구단주	당신보다 똑똑한 사람들과 어울려라	Surround yourself with people smarter than you.
브레드 앤더슨	베스트 바이 CEO	당신이 어떤 직위에 있느냐 보다 어떤 사람인지를 기억해라	Remember who you are, not what.
스티브 발머	마이크로소프트 CEO	인재 채용에 가장 역점을 두라	Make hiring a top priority
캐럴 바츠	오토데스크 CEO	당신이 뭘 할 수 없다고 생각한다면, 정말 못하게 될 것이다	If you think you can' t, you' re right.
마크 베니오프	세일즈베스닷컴 CEO	고객이 당신의 제품을 광고하고 다니게끔 만들어라	Make your customers your sales force.
리처드 브론슨	버진그룹 회장	실수를 저지른 사람이어도 두 번째 기회는 줘라	When people screw up, give them a second chance.
포 브론슨	작가	아내와 늘 상의하라	Check with the wife.
워런 버핏	버크셔 해서웨이 회장	당신이 둘일 수는 없다	There can' t be two yours.

이름	직업 또는 직책	좌우명 (한글)	좌우명 (영어)
존 체임버스	시스코시스템스 CEO	고객을 항상 행복하게 만들어야 한다	The customer should always be happy.
사이먼 쿠퍼	리츠 컬튼 대표	할 수 있다고 자꾸 말하면, 결국 행동으로 이어지게 마련이다	He who say sit, does it.
마크 큐번	HD 공동창업자	고객을 당신의 주인인 것처럼 대접하라. 왜냐하면 그건 사실이니까	Treat your customers like they own you, because they do.
짐 굿나잇	SAS CEO	탁상공론에 머물지 말고 행동하라	Get out from behind your desk.
앤디 그로브	전 인텔 회장	지나치게 의심이 많은 사람만이 살아남는다	Only the paranoid survive.
미레유 길리아노	클리크 CEO	하루에 한번쯤은 머리를 여유롭게 비우는 시간을 가져라	Once a day, take some "beach time"
칼루스 구티에레즈	미국 상무부장관, 전 켈로그 CEO	당신보다 뭔가 더 대단한 것을 믿어라	Believe in something bigger than yourself.
칼 아이칸	전문 투자자	사람을 판단할 때는 특히 당신 자신을 판단할 때는 행운과 진짜 실력을 구분할 줄 알아야 한다	Don' t confuse luck with skill when judging others, and especially when judging yourself.
폴 제이콥스	퀄컴 CEO	관습적인 룰을 거슬러 가라	Conventional wisdom is always wrong.
제럴딘 레이번	옥시전미디어 회장	경쟁자의 성공을 따라하려 하지 마라	You shall not covet your competitor' s success.
셸리 레저러스	오길비앤매더 회장	어떤 사업적 성공도 행복보다 중요할 수는 없다	Besuness can' t trump happiness.
스콧 맥닐리	선마이크로시스템 CEO	항상 다른 이들과 나누고 공유해라	Share and share alike
앤 멀케이	제록스 회장	고객과 마주 대하는 시간을 가져라	Get face time with the customers.
한스 올로브올슨	볼보자동차 부회장 겸 포드자동차 최고 마케팅책임자	타협의 범위를 넓혀라	Maximize the compromises.
딕 파슨스	타임워너 회장	뿌린 대로 거둔다	Whatever a man sows, that shall he also reap.
질 프레스	토요타자동차 USA 대표	당신은 고객의 종이라는 걸 절대 잊어서는 안 된다	Never, ever forget that your are a servant.
폴 프레슬어	캡 CEO	당신의 배짱을 믿어라	Learn to trust your gut.
헥터 루이스	AMD CEO	해결사가 되라	Be a problem-solver.

이름	직업 또는 직책	좌우명 (한글)	좌우명 (영어)
스리바츠 삼파트	맥아피 창업자	충성심은 명석한 두뇌만큼 중요하다	Loyalty counts as much as smarts.
아이번 사이던버그	버라이전 회장	열심히 일하는 사람에게 문이 열린다	Hard work opens doors
조지 셔힌	지벨시스템스 CEO	앞으로 나서는 사람이 되라	Be the person who steps up.
램 슈리럼	구글 이사회 멤버	과거에 뭘 했는지 모르는 사람은 과거의 실수를 반복하기 쉽다	Those who don' t know their own history are doomed to repeat it.
스텐 시그먼	싱귤러 와이어리스 CEO	제대로 평가된 것만이 제대로 관리될 수 있는 법이다	What gets measured gets managed.
러셀 시먼스	데프잼레코드 공동창업자	받지만 말고 주기 시작해라	Quit taking, start giving.
엘리엇 스피처	전 뉴욕주 검찰총장	직접 말할 수 있는 것을 글로 쓰지 마라. 행동으로 보여줄 수 있는 것을 말로만 표시하지 마라. 그리고 중요한 일은 절대 E-mail로 하지 마라	Never write when you can talk. Never talk when you can nod. And never put anything in E-mail.
에드 젠더	모토로라 회장	성공의 정점에 올랐다고 생각될 때 사업을 과감하게 재정비하라	At the height of success, break your business.

3 An Interview Model for a Hotel Clerk

▣ 호텔 직원 입사 인터뷰

A : Hello, Miss Kim. My name is Kyungho Lee. Have a seat, please.
(안녕하세요 미스 김. 저는 이경호입니다. 앉으세요.)

B : Thank you. (감사합니다.)

A : Would you like something drink? (마실 것 좀 드실래요?)

B : Thanks a lot. (감사합니다.)

A : Are you ready to interview? (이제 인터뷰하실 준비가 됐습니까?)

B : Yes, I'm ready. (예, 준비되었습니다.)

A : Let's start the interview with some questions. Where were you born?
(이제 몇 가지 질문으로 시작하겠습니다. 어디에서 태어나셨습니까?)

B : I was born in Seoul. (저는 서울에서 태어났습니다.)

A : Are you married? (결혼은 하셨습니까?)

B : No, I'm not married yet. (아뇨, 아직은 결혼하지 않았습니다.)

A : Do you live alone? (그럼 혼자 사세요?)

B : No, I live with my family. (아닙니다. 가족과 함께 삽니다.)

A : How many members are there in your family? (가족은 몇 명입니까?)

B : There are five of us. (모두 다섯명입니다.)

A : Are you the eldest? (장남이십니까?)

B : Yes, I have a younger brother and a younger sister.
(남동생 한 명과 여동생 한 명이 있습니다.)

A : What do you do for a living? (무엇을 하십니까?)

B : I'm a student. I will graduate this coming February.
(저는 학생입니다. 이번 2월에 졸업합니다.)

A : What school are you attending? (어느 학교에 다시십니까?)

B : I attend Hangook College in Seoul. (저는 서울에 있는 한국대학에 다닙니다.)

A : What is your major? (전공은 무엇입니까?)

B : I'm majoring in business adminisration. (경영학을 전공하고 있습니다.)

A : How are your scores at the college? (학교 성적은 어떻습니까?)

B : I have an A average. (평균 A입니다.)

A : Oh, really? You are an excellent student. (그래요? 매우 뛰어난 학생이군요.)

B : Thank you. (감사합니다.)

A : By the way, why did you choose our company?
(그런데, 왜 우리 회사를 선택하셨습니까?)

B : Because there is a good chance for my advancement.
(저의 발전을 위한 좋은 기회이기 때문입니다.)

A : What do you think a job is? (직업이란 어떤 거라고 생각하세요?)

B : I think a job is a way to develop myself and to maintain my livelihood.
(저는 직업이란 자신을 발전시키고 우리 생활을 유지하는 하나의 방법이라고 생각합니다.)

A : Why do you choose to work as a hotel clerk?
(왜 호텔 직원이 되려고 하십니까?)

B : I am outgoing, and I have been interested in hotel since I was young. I like to work in front of the house such as front desk and outlet etc.
(저는 성격이 외향적이어서 어렸을 때부터 호텔에 관심이 많았습니다. 프론터 데스크나 아울렛 등 건물의 앞 쪽에서 일하고 싶습니다.)

A : Can you work overtime, nights, weekends and so on?
(시간외 근무, 야간근무, 주말근무 같은 것도 할 수 있습니까?)

B : I am willing to do. (기꺼이 할 수 있습니다.)

A : What do you think your strong points and weak points are?
(당신의 장점과 단점이 무엇이라고 생각하세요?)

B : I think my strong point is that I mix with others well, and my weak point is that I am rather indecisive.
(저의 장점은 제가 다른 사람들과 잘 어울린다는 것이고, 단점은 다소 우유부단하다는 것입니다.)

A : What do you think about your attitude towards job?
(직업에 대한 당신의 태도는 어떻습니까?)

B : I always do my best to complete my work.
(저는 항상 제 일을 완수할 수 있도록 최선을 다합니다.)

A : Do you have any special conditions that you would like the company to take into consideration?
(회사에서 특별히 고려해주었으면 하는 어떤 특별한 조건이 있습니까?)

B : Nothing special. (특별한 것이 없습니다.)

A : I'm glad to meet you. I'm deeply impressed with your attitude towards job. However, we have some other applicants who must be interviewed before I make a decision. You will be contacted sometime next week if you are hired.
(만나서 반가웠습니다. 직업에 대한 당신의 태도에 깊은 인상을 받았습니다. 그렇지만 우리가 결정을 내리기 전에 인터뷰해야 할 다른 신청자들이 있습니다. 만약 당신으로 결정을 한다면 다음 주쯤에 연락해 드리겠습니다.)

B : Thank you. I hope to work with you. (감사합니다. 채용되기를 희망합니다.)

4 Food & Beverage Terms

(1) Category 중심

⊙ Meals

brunch(아침겸 점심)
luncheon/lunch(점심)
restaurant(정식식당)
cafeteria(셀프서비스식당)
dining room/place(호텔 등의 식당)
buffet(뷔페)
hotdog stand(핫도그 가게)
cocktail bar/lounge(칵테일전문바)
á la carte(일품요리, 주문식단)
spaghetti(스파게티)
chef's suggestion(조리장이 권유하는 요리)
table d'hôte(정식요리)
today's special(오늘의 특별요리)
appetizer(전채)
main dish(주 요리 meat/seafood)
head cook, chef(주방장)
rice/ steamed rice(밥)
noodles (국수)
dumpling(만두)

⊙ Meat(육류)

beef(쇠고기 c.f. cow)
pork(돼지고기 c.f. pig)
mutton/lamb(양고기 c.f. sheep)
chicken(닭고기 c.f. cock/hen)
turkey(칠면조)
duck(오리)
pheasant(꿩)
rare(고기를 거의 익히지 않은)
medium(고기를 반쯤 익힌)
well-done(고기를 완전히 익힌
fillet(소, 돼지의 등심살)
veal(송아지고기 c.f. calf)
sirloin(소의 허리 상부의 살)
rib steak(소갈비)
rump(소의 엉덩이살)
T-bone steak(T자형의 뼈가 붙어있는 것)
roast beef(불고기)
minced beef(쇠고기를 다진 것)
pork chop(고기가 붙어있는 돼지갈비)
smoked ham(훈제 햄)
pig's feet(족발)

⊙ Eggs(달걀 요리 종류)

soft boiled(흰자만 익힌 반숙 달걀)
hard boiled(노른자까지 익힌 완숙 달걀)
sunny-side up(달걀 한쪽 흰자만 익힌 것)
over easy(양쪽 흰자를 익힌 달걀)
over hard(노른자까지 모두 익힌 달걀)
turned over(양면을 후라이한 달걀)
scrambled(휘저어서 익힌 달걀)
poached(깨어서 끓는 물에 떨어뜨려 삶는 달걀(수란)

⊙ Spice(양념)

salt(소금)
vinegar(초, 식초)
mustard(겨자)
pepper(후추)
ginger(생강)
garlic(마늘)
condiment(양념, 향신료)
ketchup(케찹)
mayonnaise(마요네즈)
sesame oil(참기름)
soybean sauce(간장)

⊙ Drinks(음료)

decaffeinated coffee(카페인 없는 커피)
black coffee(크림과 설탕을 넣지 않은 커피)
tea with (a slice of) lemon(레몬티)
without gas/non-carbonated(탄산없음)
with gas/carbonated(탄산있음)
noodle(국수)
Chinese noodle(라면)
buckwheat noodle(메밀국수)
coke(콜라)
diet coke(다이어트 콜라)
coke caffeine free(카페인 없는 콜라)
beverage(커피, 홍차 등의 음료수)
cheer/ bottoms up/ toast(건배!)
whisky and water(위스키에 물 섞은 것)
lager beer(병맥주)
draft beer(생맥주)
dark beer(흑맥주)
light beer(라이트 맥주)
ginger ale(생강음료수)
mineral water(약수)
vintage wine(고급포도주)
on the rocks(얼음에 띄어 놓은)
dry(씁쌀한 맛이 나는)
semi-dry(약간 씁쌀한 맛이 나는)
extra-dry(매우 씁쌀한 맛이 나는)
straight(얼음, 물 없이 원래의 술만 마시는 것)
whiskey(보리, 귀리, 밀 등이 원료, 발효 양조하고 이것을 증류하여 만든 것)
brandy(포도, 사과, 체리 등의 과일의 발효액을 증류하여 만든 것)
cognac(프랑스산 브랜디로 Cognac지방에서 유래함)
champagne(샴페인, 프랑스 상파뉴 지방이 1급 원산지)
gin(대맥, 호밀 등의 향료 물질을 첨가하여 증류한 것)
vodka(무색, 무취, 무향의 증류주. 러시아 슬라브족의 국민주)
rum(사탕수수나 고구마로 만든 것. 자메이카산이 최고품)

⊙ Ways of Cook(요리방법)

fry(기름에 튀기는 것)
bake(빵, 과자를 불에 직접 대지 않고 굽는 것)
poach(끓는 액체에 넣고 데치기)
roast(기름칠을 하여 굽거나 볶는 것)
stew(은근한 불로 끓이기, 찌기)
boil(끓이기, 삶기)
braise(pan에 담아 볶다)
smoke(훈제하다)

raw(날 것)
mash(짓이기다)
marinate(양념에 담가 절이다)
mince(잘게 저미다)
broil/grill(생선, 고기를 직접 불을 쬐어 석쇠에 굽는 것)

⦿ Sea foods(해산물)

salmon(연어)
eel(뱀장어)
tuna(참치)
trout(송어)
cuttlefish(뼈오징어)
squid(말려서 먹는 오징어)
lobster(바다가재)
caviar(철갑상어 알젓)
carp(잉어)
oyster(굴)
mackerel(고등어)
mackerel pike(꽁치)
cod(대구)
scallop(가리비)
flatfish(가자미)
herring(청어)
seaweed(해초)
clam(대합)
brown seaweed(미역)
crab(게)
anchovy(멸치)
laver, green seaweed(김)
abalone(전복)
shrimp(새우)
shark(상어)
octopus(문어)
snail(달팽이)
hair-tail(갈치)
sea cucumber(해삼)
sardine(정어리)

⦿ 채소류 및 과일

cucumber(오이)
eggplant(가지)
green beans(강낭콩)
pea(완두콩)
lettuce(상치)
sesame(깨)
radish(무)
cabbage(양배추)
red pepper(고추)
green pepper(피망)
spinach(시금치)
parsley(파슬리)
Chinese cabbage(배추)
green onion(파)
leek(부추)
mugwort(쑥)
mushroom(버섯)
bamboo shoot(죽순)
asparagus(아스파라거스)
broccoli(브로콜리)
celery(샐러리)
carrot(당근)
beet(사탕무우)
apricot(살구)
chestnut(밤)
raisin(건포도)
fig(무화과나무)
crown daisy(쑥갓)

walnut(호도)
grapefruit(자몽)
plum(플럼, 서양자두)
muskmelon(서양참외)
bean sprout(콩나물)
ginkgo nut(은행)
tangerine(탠져린, 귤의 일종)
avocado(아보카도)
green onion/scallion(파)
lotus root(연근)
sweet potatoes(고구마)
pumpkin(호박)
prune(서양자두)
watermelon(수박)
peach(복숭아)
cantaloupes(참외)
kiwis(키위)
muskmelon(참외)
persimmon(감)
braken(고사리)
cauliflower(꽃양배추)
sesame leaves(깻잎)
squash(애호박)

(2) 알파벳 순

Age 증류수의 숙성과정에서 술통 속에 저장한 기간을 말하며, 포도주의 Vintage와 비슷하다.

A La ~풍의,~식의,~을 곁들인

á la carte 일품요리(메뉴 중 자기가 좋아 하는 요리를 선택하여 주문하는 형식)

A La Mode 각종 파이류에 아이스크림을 얹어서 제공하는 일종의 후식
1. 유행하는
2. 아이스크림을 얹은
3. 현대풍의
e.g. apple pie a la mode : 아이스크림을 얹은 애플파이

American French Dressing 드레싱의 일종으로 계란. 식초. 샐러드. 마늘. 겨자. 레몬, 주스 등을 재료로 한 드레싱. 정통 French Dressing과는 다른 Cream Type

American Service 음식을 주방에서 미리 접시에다 1인분씩 준비해 두었다가 고객에게 제공하는 식당 서비스형식으로 신속한 서비스에 적합하고, 고급식당이 아닌 일반식당에서 널리 이용되며, late Service라고도 함.

Aperitif 식전에 식욕을 증진시키기 위하여 마시는 술로서 각종 칵테일 및 Aperitif Wine 이 있다

Arm Chair 팔걸이 의자

Arm Towel 서비스 타월 (service towel) 종사원이 팔에 걸쳐 사용하는 서비스용 냅킨

Bacon and Eggs American Breakfast

Banquet 연회

Banquet Event Order 연회행사를 각 관련부서에 알리는 연회행사통보서

Bar 주류를 위주로 하여 영업하는 장소

Bar Boy Bar에서 필요한 과일 . 주스. 술. 얼음 등과 같은 품목을 Bartender에게 공급하는 종사원

Boiled Eggs 삶은 계란

Brandy 좁은 의미로는 포도를 발효, 증류한 술을 말하며, 넓은 의미로는 모든 과실류의 발효액을 증류한 알콜 성분이 강한 술의 총칭

Bread Basket 빵을 담는 바구니

Brunch 아침과 점심 사이에 하는 식사를 말한다. 아침(breakfast)과 점심 (lunch)의 합성어. 주로 10~12시 사이에 간단한 음식으로 제공된다.

Bus Boy 접객원 또는 주방 일을 도와주는 보조자

Cafeteria 음식물을 손님 자신이 날라다 먹기 편리하도록 counter Table 에 있어 직접 요금을 지급하고 이용하는 Self Service식의 간이식당

Call Liquor 고객에 의해서 요청되어진 특별한 상표의 주류

Camembert Cheese Soft Cheese의 일종으로 프랑스의 Normandy 지방의 Camembert(까망베르) 마을에서 처음으로 만들어졌으며, 먹을 때 외피를 벗겨 먹는 것이 보통인데, 이것은 자극적인 냄새가 너무 강하고, 과숙한 경우에는 Ammonia 냄새도 나기 때문.

Canape 빵을 잘게 여러 가지 모양으로 만들어 그 위에 각종 가공된 음식물을 얹어서 한입에 먹을 수 있게 만든 요리

Captain 업장에서 웨이터나 웨이트리스들을 통솔하며, 어떤 한 Section을 담당하여 주문을 받는 주임급 직원

Carafe 하우스 와인을 담아서 제공하는 Decanter

Carte de Jour 그 날의 특별메뉴(daily special menu)

Cashier 회계계원

Caster Set 테이블에 놓는 소금과 후추 세트를 지칭한다

Catering 식음료 부서에 속하면서 일종의 출장요리

Caviar 철갑상어(sturgeon)의 알

Charlet 최상급의 보르드 와인을 부를 때 사용되는 용어

Chaser 주정이 강한 술을 마실 때 곁들어 마시는 청량음료

Chateau Briand 소의 등뼈 양쪽에 붙여 있는 가장 연한 안심의 머리 부분을 말한다

Chef 식당의 주방장(kitchen chief)

Chef de Rang 식당 서비스 조직에 있어서 일개 구역(약5개 식탁이 놓인곳)을 담당하는 종사원

Chilled water 식당에서 고객의 Water Glass에 따라 주는 냉수(ice water)

Chinaware 각종 도자기 집기류

Cocktail Lounge 라운지(lounge)옆에 바(bar)를 설비하여 양주에서 소프트 드링크까지 이른바 음료를 마시면서 담화하는 넓고 큰 방.

Collation 간단한 식사나 간식

Complaints 고객의 불만이나 불평사항

Complimentary 호텔의 객실 및 식음료를 무료로 제공

Compote 맑게 만든 숙실과일 일종 (설탕 절인 과일)

Condiment 조리에 쓰이는 각종 양념류의 총칭

Continental Breakfast Juice, Toast, Roll or Sweet Roll, Coffee(tea or milk)로 구성된 식사, 메뉴에 계란이 곁들이지 않은 조식, 음료(커피. 홍차. 주스. 코코아. 밀크)와 butter로만 이루어진 식사

Continental plan 유럽식 아침식사로 보통 커피 또는 우유와 빵 . 치즈가 제공

Corkage 손님이 가져 온 술병에 대한 서비스 룰 (마개를 뽑아 주는 서비스 룰)

Corkage charge 호텔 식당에 있어서 그 식당의 술을 구매치 않고 고객이 가지고 온 술을 마실 때 마개를 뽑아 주는 봉사료

Covers 업장에서 음료와 음식을 시키는 고객의 수 (음료만 주문할 경우에는 cover로 치지 않는다)

Cradle 적포도주를 제공할 때 쓰이는 바구니

Cuisine 요리 혹은 조리법

Cutlet 얇게 저민 고기나 생선에 밀가루 . 계란. 빵가루 등을 묻혀서 Fried 한 요리

Daily menu 식당의 전략메뉴라 할 수 있는 이 식단은 매일 시장에서 나오는 특별재료를 사입하여 조리장의 기술을 최대로 발휘하여 고객의 식욕을 자극할 수 있는 메뉴

Daily special menu 주방장이 제공하는 그날의 특별메뉴

Danish Blue 덴마크산 푸른 곰팡이 치즈

Danish Pastry 덴마크식 빵으로 반죽을 유지로 싸서 퍼프 패스트리(puff pastry)처럼 밀고 접기를 반복하여 굽는 빵

Decanter 각종 음료를 담는 용기로서 Cocktail Decanter, Wine Decanter 가 있다

Deluxe Restaurant 고급호텔에 부수되어 있는 Main Restaurant이나 격이 높고 품위가 있는 고급식당

Dessert Wine 주(main)식사가 끝나고 디저트(dessert)를 먹을 때 같이 먹는 와인(wine)으로서 주로 sweet wine이 쓰이며, port wine, sweet sherry wine, sweet red wine, sweet white wine 등이 많이 애용

Dining Room 식당을 운영하는 시간이 제한되어 있어 대개의 경우 아침식사시간은 영업을 하지 않고 점심과 저녁식사만을 제공하면서 주로 정찬을 판매하는 식당

Dessert 식후에 먹는 음식으로서 Main course를 먹고 나면 Dessert를 제공한다. 주로 Sweet, Savoury 및 Fruit의 3가지 요소가 포함된 것을 제공

DNP 게시판에 부착하지 마라 (Do Not Post)

Do Not Disturb 호텔의 객실에서 종업원이나 손님의 출입을 제한하는 표시로서 손님이 문에 걸어 두는 표지에 쓰는 용어

Dolci 이태리 음식에서의 후식

Doyley 작은 냅킨으로서 식탁 위에 깔고 세팅을 할 때 쓰는, 약간 무늬가 있는 것과 물, 주스, 맥주 등을 serve할 때 밑받침으로 사용되는 원형의 도일리가 있음.

Draft beer 제조과정에서 발효균을 살균하지 않은 생맥주 (lager beer)

Dressed Food 음식상품으로서의 가치를 높이기 위하여 드레서(dresser)에 의해 예쁘게 장식되고 정리한 음식. Dressing sauce의 일종으로 모든 샐러드에 곁들이거나 혼합해서 고객에게 제공

Dry 주조상의 용어로 드라이라고 할 때는 당분이 없다는 뜻이며 Dry Wine 이라고 할 때는 단맛이 없는 포도주를 의미

Duchess Potatoes 삶은 감자를 달걀노른자와 함께 휘젓고 패스트리 튜브를 이용해 모양 있게 짜 놓은 후 살라멘터에서 노릇하게 구워 낸 감자요리의 일종

Duchesse 으깬 감자요리에 계란노른자를 섞어 만든 것.

Dumpling 밀가루나 삶은 달걀에 기름이나 양념을 매합하여 끓는 물에서 만들어 내는 요리

Dutch Coffee 물을 사용하여 3시간 이상 추출한 독특하고 향기 좋은 커피

entrée 정식의 여러 코스 중 줌심이 되는 요리로, 쇠고기. 송아지고기. 돼지고기. 양고기 뿐만 아니라 생선이나 새고기 종류도 식사 코스의 중심이 된다면 앙트레로 조리할 수 있다. 이외에도 쌀이 주식인 곳에서는 밥. 국수 빵 등이 모두 앙트레.

Equipment 식당, 주방, 연회행사에 필요한 각종 장비

Espresso 이탈리아식 커피추출법으로 농도를 진하게 추출해내는 방법이다.

Executive Chef 모든 주방장(chef)을 지휘, 통솔하는 부방부장으로 실제적인 조리

(cooking)보다는 메뉴계획이라든가 인사 등 주방부서의 행정적인 면을 담당

F&B(Food & Beverage) 식료. 음료를 통칭하는 말

Filet 육류나 생선의 뼈나 지방질을 추려낸 상태

Flat Ware 테이블에 쓰이는 은기물류의 총칭(cutlery)

Float 술의 비중을 이용하여 한 가지 술에 따른 술을 혼잡하지 않고 위에 붓거나 칵테일에 아이스크림 등을 띄울 때 쓰이는 명칭

Free pick-up Service 무료로 호텔 등에서 제공하는 서비스

French Service 주방장이나 요리사가 고객 앞에서 직접 요리하여 서브하는 방식

Fried Eggs (turned over, sunny-side up) 후라이 에그(양면을 구운, 한면만 구운)

Gouda Cheese 네덜란드 남부에 위치한 가우다 근교에서 200여년 전부터 만들어진 것으로 지방 함량이 높으며, 외피는 적색으로 염색한다. 이 치즈는 살균시키지 않은 우유를 가지고 만든 Sweet Curd Cheese로서 Semi-Soft에서 Hard Cheese까지 있다

Gourmet 식도 또는 식도락가

Great Wine 포도주를 만들어서 15년 이상 저장하여 50년 이내에 마시는 와인을 말한다

Grill 숯불이나 가스 혹은 전기복사열 같은 불꽃 위에 철판을 달궈 익히는 철판구이나 석쇠구이 또는 그릴을 위주로 하는 일품요리식당

Hard Boiled Eggs 완숙 계란

Host bar 객실 내에 설치되어 있으며, Mini Bar라고 함

Hotel Personnel 호텔이나 모텔 등과 같은 숙박업소에 종사하는 종사원

Hotelier 호텔업자 또는 호텔지배인. 관리인. 소유주를 총칭

Huse wine 호텔이 영업신장을 위하여 정한 기획와인으로 대체적으로 저렴한 상품을 Glass 단위로 판매할 수 있는 와인

Junk food '쓰레기', '잡동사니' 의 의미. 아주 불명예스러운 이름을 갖게 된 이 음식들은 칼로리는 높으나 영양가가 낮은 스낵류의 식품이나 인스턴트 식품을 말한다. 캔디, 포테토 칩, 초콜릿 같이 설탕, 기름 등의 함량이 높아 몸에 유익하지 않은 살찌는 음식들을 가리킴.

La Newburgr 계란 노른자, 크림, 와인 등으로 만든 Sauce

Lager Beer 제조과정에서 발효균을 살균하여 병에 넣은 맥주를 말한다 (draft beer)

Linen 테이블 클로스와 냅킨. 드레스 등을 총칭하여 부르는말

Linen-Room 호텔의 리넨류를 저장하면서 필요한 제품을 Room Maid나 식당관계자들에게 제공

Luncheon 오찬을 뜻하며, 아침과 저녁 중간에 먹는 가벼운 식사를 말한다. 대개 3~4 코스로 구성되어 있다. 즉 수프(soup), 후식(dessert), 음료(coffee or tea)

Main Dish 주요리(main course)식사단계 중 가장 으뜸이 되는 일명 앙트레(entrée)

Mashed Potato 삶아서 직이긴 감자와 버터. 우유를 섞어서 만든 음식

Medium 중간으로 익힌 요리, 알맞게 익힌 요리

Medium Rare Rare보다는 좀 더 익히며, Medium보다는 좀 덜 익힌 것으로, 역시 자르면 피가 보이도록 하여야 한다. 조리시간은 약 3~4 분 정도이고, 고기 내부의 온도는 55℃ 정도

Menu Tent Card 천막식으로 접어서 식탁에 세워 놓은 메뉴카드

Mignon 쇠고기의 안심 끝부분을 스테이크용으로 토막 내서 베이컨을 감은 것 (예: filet mignon)

Mini Bar 고객의 편의를 위하여 간단한 주류, 음료를 이용할 수 있도록 객실에 준비되어 있는 작은 바

MIP(most important person) VIP(very important person)보다 더 중요한 고객

Order 주문, 지시, 명령. 음식을 주문하는 것

Order Slip 웨이터가 작성하는 식음료의 주문전표

Order Taker 식당이나 룸 서비스에 있어서 주문을 받는 사람

Over Easy 계란 한 쪽이 살짝 익으면 엎어서 다른 한쪽을 익혀 양쪽의 흰자만 약간 익힌 것.

Over Hard 계란요리의 일종인 Fried Egg 의 요리방업으로 흰자와 노른자를 모두 익힌 것.

Over Heat 석쇠 위에 고기를 얹어 직접 열을 받게 하여 뒤집어 가며 굽는 조리법

Over Medium Fried Egg의 요리방법으로 흰자는 완전히 익고, 노른자는 약간 익힌 것.

Over Sold 판매초과

Plate Service 식당 서비스 중 가장 간단하고 빠른 서비스 방법으로 주방에서 음식을 미리 접시(plate)에 담에 놓은 것을 접객원들이 날라다가 서브하는 형식으로 비교적 숙련된 종사원을 필요로 하지 않기 때문에 대중식당에서 많이 이용

Reception Desk 일반적으로 고급식당의 입구에 높여 있는 단이 높은 책상으로서 주로 접객수장이나 리셉션니스트가 고객의 예약을 받거나 식당에 오는 예약고객의 안내를 위해서 예약장부 전화기 고객명부 등을 비치하여 놓고 사용

Reception Hostess 고객을 영접하고 등록시키는 직무를 책임지는 여자

Receptionist 레스토랑에서 고객을 영접 예약 등록하고, table arrange 등의 직무를 책임지는 사람

Recipe 조리나 칵테일의 내용물과 조리방법을 세밀하게 기록한 것으로 주로 카드를 이용하여 호텔이나 식당에서 표준상품의 제품지침서로 사용한다

Reservation 숙박뿐만 아니라 식사 연회 등도 포함되는 예약으로서 성명, 객실형 요금, 도착일시, 숙박일수, 직업, 연락처, 명수 등을 편지 전화 전보 팩스 등에 의하여 적어도 도착 3일 전 경에 도착될 수 있도록 예약을 해둘 필요가 있음.

Reservation Clerk 호텔 투숙계의 객실사용에 관한 예약업무를 담당하는 객실담당

직원으로 대형 호텔의 경우는 룸 클럭에서 독립되어 있으나 작은 호텔은 룸 클럭이 예약업무를 수행함

Reservation Confirmation 호텔의 시설을 사용하기 전에 예약이 확실히 되어 있는지를 확인하는 것

Room Service 객실에 투숙 중인 고객의 편의를 위해 식사. 음료 등을 객실에 운반하는 서비스를 행하거나 영업과 관계된 고객의 요청사하을 대행하는 호텔식음부의 영업부서

Scrambled Eggs 풀어 볶은 계란 (계란 2개 반 + 우유 큰 스푼을 섞어 저은 후 미리 버터를 녹여 놓은 프라이팬에 붓고 약한 불로 저어 만든 계란요리)

Season Rate 계절별 할인요금. 비수기 판매정책으로서 호텔에서 고객의 이용률이 적은 계절에 한해 공표요금 할인하여 요금을 적용하기도 하는데, 이러한 경우의 할인요금

Seasonal Menu 한 계절에 맞게 작성된 차림표로서 그 계절의 대표적인 요리를 중심으로 구성

Service Charge 구미의 호텔이나 레스토랑에서 고객이 종업원의 서비스에 대하여 팁을 지불하는 것.

Service Elevator 종사원 승강기이며, 룸 서비스와 하우스키핑 및 엘리베이터 영선 기타 목적으로 사용하는 호텔 종사원의 서비스용 승강기인데, 고객의 눈에 잘 띄지 않는 곳에 위치한다고 하여 Back Elevator하고도 함.

Service Spoon and Fork 일반적인 디너 스푼이나 포크보다 크며, 접객원들이 음식을 덜어 내거나 서브할 때 사용하는 스푼과 포크

Service Station 영업에 필요한 모든 준비물 (기물. 소모품. 메뉴 등)을 비치하여 접객 서비스를 신속하게 할 수 있도록 식당내부의 적절한 장소에 고정시켜 종사원들만 사용하는 비품함

Service Towel 식당접객원들이 사용하는 팔에 걸치는 수건으로 암 타월 (arm towel)이라고도 함

Service Wagon 고객의 요리를 운반 또는 serve 할 때 사용하는 이동운반차이며, 영업 전에 Arm Towel, Serving Gear (spoon&fork),Tray를 비치

Set-up 얼음과 컵 그리고 비알콜성 혼합용 물질은 고객이 집이나 다른 곳에서 사온 술과 함께 비교적 싼 값으로 테이블에 제공하는 것으로, 흔히 레스토랑에서 술의 판매가 금지된 지역의 경우에 사용하는 방법

Severy 식당영업을 위한 식기실 혹은 상 차리는방

Shift 근무조, 근무시간

Show plate 식탁을 차릴 때 고객좌석의 중심을 표시하기 위한 장식접시로서 그 위에 냅킨을 올려놓는다. 대개 동이나 놋쇠로 만들며, 특별 제작품이 없을 때는 앙트레 접시로 대용하여 테이블에 놓는다.

Side Board 더미 웨이터(dummy waiter)라고도 불리는 이 사이드 보드는 시간당 고객의 서비스를 위하여 그 식사시간에 필요한 예비기물(식탁기물. 린넨. 메뉴. 접시 등)들을 준비하는데 접시를 데우는 시설이 가설되어 있는 것도 있다

Silver Ware 식당기물 중에서 은으로 도금이 되어 있는 식기류

Skipper 객실 값을 안내고 도망간 사람이며, 정당한 퇴숙 절차를 이행하지 않고 떠나 버리거나, 식당에서 식대 등을 지불하지 않거나 지불약속을 하지 않고 도주해 버리는 고객

Skipper Bill 고객이 호텔 이용시 금액을 미납하거나 도주하였을 경우 담당지배인이 부서장의 결제를 받아서 배상에서 처리하는 형태의 빌

Snack Bar 흔히 서서 식사를 하는 간이식당 counter service와 self service 형식으로 제공

Straight(up) 얼음이 없이 마시는것

Sunny-side up 계란을 한 면만 익힌 후 살라맨더(salamander)에 잠시 넣어서 윗면을 덥혀서 요리

Table Cloth 식탁보

Table D'Hote 정식 (행사주관자인 host의 의견에 따라 정해진 코스대로 진행되는 음식)

Table Silver 식탁용 기물 혹은 은기물로서 스푼. 포크, 칼, 버터칼

Table Skirt 오르되브르(hor d'oeuvre) 테이블이나 뷔페 테이블(buffet table) 옆 부분에 보이지 않도록 혹은 장식으로 둘러치는 식탁용 치마로 색깔이 아름다운 주름치마를 많이 사용

Turned-over Fried Egg의 요리방법 중의 하나로 오버 이지(over easy) 오버 미디엄(over medium), 오버 하드(over hard) 등이 있음

Valet Service 호텔의 세탁소(laundry)나 주차장(parking lot)에서 고객을 위해 호텔종업원이 직접적으로 고객의 일을 대행하는 서비스

VIP(very important person) 중요한 고객 또는 지명도가 높은 고객, 경우에 따라서는 귀찮은 손님도 해당된다. 특별한 주의 및 관심을 요하는 고객 또는 그 예약

Wagon Service 요리를 서비스방식으로 작은 차가 달린 웨곤에 요리를 싣고 서비스를 행한다. 경우에 따라서는 고객 앞에서 간단한 요리를 행할 수도 있다

Waiter's Knife 접객원들이 식당 서비스를 할 때 휴대하는 기물

Walk-in Guest 예약을 하지 않고 그 호텔에 투숙하는 고객

Well-Done 많이 익힌 스테이크요리

Wine Cradle 와인을 뉘어놓는 손잡이가 달린 바구니 혹은 와인 바스켓

Answers

Chapter 1 Reservation & Greeting

Unit 1 Telephone Reservation

▣ Key expressions

1. What time are you open for lunch?
2. I'd like to reserve a table for tomorrow evening.
3. There is one table left by the window.
4. May I have your name and phone number please?
5. I'm really sorry, but we're fully booked.
6. Is there anything else I can do for you?
7. How many persons in your party?
8. In what name shall I make a reservation?
9. What time do you have in mind?
10. What can I do for you?

▣ Grammar

1. Shall I bring your appetizers first?
2. Shall I make you a cocktail?
3. Shall I take your orders?
4. Shall I bring your bill?
5. Shall I pay the check right now?

▣ Review & Exercises

3. Exercises

1) a. for b. on c. by d. for e. for, at, for f. In g. for
2) can I do for you / reserve a table / fully-booked / will be available / mind / anyway / have a change to serve / for your calling

▣ Restaurant Quiz

1 sour 2 bill of fare 3 cooked very little

Unit 2 Changing, Confirming & Cancelling the Reservation

▣ Key expressions

1. What time should we expect you?
2. Thank you for calling, sir.

3. How about tomorrow evening?

4. Thank you for letting us know.

5. We hope we may serve you next time.

6. I must cancel the table for tonight.

7. Under what name did you make a reservation?

8. If you change or cancel your reservation, please let us know.

9. Please book a table commanding a good view.

10. We look forward to seeing you tomorrow evening.

▣ Grammar

1.

bright	brighter – brightest	easy	easier – easiest
good	better – best	wonderful	more wonderful – most wonderful
hot	hotter – hottest	friendly	more friendly – most friendly friendlier – friendliest
cold	colder – coldest	bad	worse – worst
healthy	healthier – healthiest	intelligent	more intelligent – most intelligent
tall	taller – tallest	sunny	sunnier – sunniest
heavy	heavier – heaviest	honest	more honest – most honest
large	larger – largest	early	earlier – earliest

주의) angry / clever / narrow / simple / friendly는 ~er 와 more, most가 모두 사용됨.

2. a. busier b. closer c. more expensive d. better e. cheaper f. not as smooth

3. 1. 9:05 2. 3:45 3. 4:30 4. 11:15 5. 7:45 6. 2:30 7. 2/12/2016

8. March twentieth two thousand seventeen

9. October twelfth, nineteen ninety-eight 10 (various)

▣ Review & Exercises

3 Exercises

1) a. about b. to c. off d. for e. In (or Under)

2) book a table for two / fully booked / How about / May I have your name / forward to seeing you

▣ Restaurant Quiz

1 beat 2 yolk 3 peel

Unit 3 Welcoming & Seating the Guest

▣ Key expressions

1. Come this way, please

2. Would you mind waiting for 20 minutes?

3. I'll be back to take your order.
4. There is a table by the aisle.
5. How would you like your steak?
6. It commands a beautiful view of the Han River.
7. How do you like this table?
8. I'll be right back in a moment, sir.
9. Why don't you have a seat in the lounge?
10. Do you have a table for two now?

■ Grammar

1. 1) an 2) the 3) a 4) an 5) a 6) the
2. 1) many 2) some, an 3) some 4) a, an 5) some 6) some 7) much 8) a
3. 1) some 2) A 3) some 4) an 5) some 6) a 7) a 8) some

■ Review & Exercises

3. Exercises

1) a. by b. by c in d. at e. in
2) (1) make a reservation / come this way / this table / would be great / right back in
   (2) have a reservation / at this moment table for you / wait for a while / have a seat / the table is ready

■ Restaurant Quiz

1. sensitive to 2. additional 3. chopped beef

Chapter 2 Order Taking & Meal Services

Unit 4 Breakfast

■ Key expressions

1. What would you like for breakfast?
2. How would you like your eggs?
3. Are you ready to order?
4. Would you like anything to drink?
5. What is today's special menu?
6. What would you like to drink, ma'am?
7. What kind of drinks do you have?
8. May I take your order?
9. Let me have the American breakfast.
10. They are not in season now.

■ Grammar

1. 1) I'll have a salad with ranch dressing. 2) I'll have the beef lasagna, please.
   3) I'll have another glass of wine. 4) I'll take the seafood platter, please.
   5) I'll have a Vodka Martini. 6) I'll have a slice of cherry pie of dessert, please.
2. 1) Is it possible to change your order? 2) Is it possible to order something unusual.
   3) Is it possible to cancel your reservation. 4) Is it possible to stay an extra day.
   5) Is it possible to connect to the Internet.

■ Review & Exercises

3. Exercises

1) a. on b. in c. away d. up

2) Pair Activity (1) What would you like for breakfast? / would you like your eggs? / Sunny-side up / No, thanks

Pair Activity (2) (various answers)

▣ Restaurant Quiz

1. tough 2. pan 3. 16 ounces

Unit 5 Lunch Key expressions

1. Are you ready to order your lunch?
2. What would you like to drink?
3. I'll be right back with it.
4. May I take your order?
5. What are today's specials?
6. May I bring something from the bar?
7. What do you recommend?
8. How about the seafood?
9. Let me order a glass of house wine, please
10. I'll be back with your drink in a moment.

▣ Grammar

2. 1) Why don't you try some dessert?

2) Why don't you order a salad.

3) Why don't you get the pasta.

4) Why don't you drink some coffee.

5) Why don't you have the steak.

6) Why don't you sample the wine.

▣ Review & Exercises

3. Exercises

1) a. in b. for c. from

2) Pair Activity (various answers)

▣ Restaurant Quiz

1. eggs 2. Over hard 3. Over easy 4. Sunny-side up

Unit 6 Dinner

▣ Key expressions

1. How do you prepare it?
2. How would you like your steak?
3. Do you want a soup or salad with that?
4. I'd like to start with the vegetable soup.
5. I can't make up my mind.
6. What's good on the menu today?
7. May I have my check, please?
8. Can you recommend some food?
9. Which soup would you like to have?
10. What is your specialty for an entrée?

▣ Grammar

1. 1) Pasta is made from flour, eggs, and salt.

2) Dressing is made from oil and vinegar.

2. 1) The tablecloth is placed on the table.
   2) The napkin is folded and placed on the side plate.
   3) The knife and fork are placed each side of the plate.
   4) The Wine glass is put above the soup spoon.
   5) The salt and pepper are put in the middle of the table.
   6) The main course plate is taken away when the main course is finished.
   7) The dessert spoon and fork are brought with the dessert menu.
   8) The flower arrangement is placed next to the salt and pepper.

▣ Restaurant English Tips

1. g 2. e 3. f 4. j 5. I 6. k 7. h 8. l 9. c 10. b 11. a 12. d

▣ Review & Exercises

3. Exercises

1) a. with b. to c. up d. on
2) is the menu / recommend some food / shrimp cocktail / have shrimp cocktail / shrimp cocktail / specialty for / like to have / would you prefer / wait a second
3) (various answers)

▣ Restaurant Quiz

1. know the menu 2. help guest order

Unit 7 Beverage & Dessert

▣ Key expressions

1. Can I get you anything else?
2. Would you like something to drink before your meal?
3. Would you recommend something popular?
4. Can I help you with your choice?
5. Take your time.
6. Will that be for here or to go, ma'am?
7. Will you please rush my order?
8. Would you like to order something to drink?
9. What kind of dressing would you like to have?
10. Would you like anything else?

▣ Grammar

1. 1) any 2) some 3) some 4) any 5) some 6) any
2. 1) Could you give me the telephone number?
   2) Could you repeat your surname?
   3) Could you spell the name of a town?

4) Could you tell me if there are any vegetarians in a group?
5) Could you confirm what time you are arriving?
6) Can you tell me how many people there are in a group?

▣ Review & Exercises

3. Exercises

1) a. with b. to c. in d. on
2) (1) (various answers)
   (2) cheeseburger / french fries / Coke / a / cake / a / icecream / coffee

▣ Restaurant Quiz

1. b.d.e 2. a 3 b. 2 c. 1

Chapter 3 More on Restaurant Services

Unit 8 Handling Complaints

▣ Key expressions

1. This is not what I ordered.
2. Would you like something else while you are waiting?
3. I'm afraid the orders got mixed up.
4. Is everything all right, sir?
5. Would you like it cooked a little more?
6. I haven't been served yet.
7. I'm sorry to have kept you waiting, sir.
8. Would you exchange it for me?
9. Will you do me a favor?
10. I'm on a low sodium diet.

▣ Grammar

1) Yes, I'll get you one.
2) Yes, I'll get you some more.
3) Yes, I'll bring you another.
4) Yes, I'll get you one.
5) Yes, I'll get you another.

▣ Review & Exercises

3. Exercises

1) a. up b. on c. of d. on
2) (various answers)

▣ Restaurant Quiz

1. White wine, Rose
2. Clockwise from the host's left

Unit 9 Paying the Bill & Goodbye

▣ Key expressions

1. Can I have the check, please?
2. This is my treat, I insist.

3. Let's go Dutch.
4. I hope you enjoyed your meal.
5. How would you like to pay, sir?
6. Do you accept Master card?
7. Which would you like to prefer, separate bill or all in one?
8. Could you sign here, please?
9. You can keep the change.
10. No tipping is our policy.

▣ Grammar

1. It's too rare, It's expected to be medium.
2. It's too tough. It's expected to be tender.
3. It's too thick. It's expected to be thin.
4. It's too noisy. It's expected to be quiet.
5. It's too spicy. It's expected to be mild.

▣ Review & Exercises

3. Exercises

1) a. go b. together c. keep d. tipping
2) Can I have the check, / Can I have the check / Let's go Dutch,

▣ Restaurant Quiz

1. Twist the bottle as you bring it up.
2. Half a glass

Unit 10 Room Services

▣ Key expressions

1. We want to have a continental breakfast for two.
2. Would you care for coffee or tea?
3. May I have your name and room number, please?
4. I'll have it sent to you immediately.
5. Please forgive the delay.
6. I'd like to reserve supper for two?
7. What kind of menu do you have?
8. You'll find a menu in the desk drawer, sir.
9. I'd like to order some champagne.
10. What time would you like it served?

▣ Grammar

1. 1) What is the weather like?
   2) What is the restaurant like?
   3) What is the local beer like?
   4) What is the beaches like?
   5) What is the music like?
   6) What is the facilities like?

▣ Review & Exercises

3. Exercises

1) a. for b. for
2) (various answers)
3) (1) May I take your order now?
   (2) What kind of menu do you have?
   (3) I'd like to reserve supper for two.
   (4) What time would you like it served?
   (5) Thank you for calling.
4) (1) May I help you,
   (2) I'd like to order some champagne.
   (3) How many bottles,
   (4) make sure they're cold.
   (5) May I have your name and room number, please?

▣ Restaurant Quiz

1. a) It's breakfast time.
2. False

Unit 12 All-in-One Restaurant Service
레스토랑 서비스영어 종합편

Activity 1 : Word Study(the top 10 useful words)

1. chef 2. compliment 3. receipt 4. mistake 5. pay 6. bill 7. meal 8. rarely 9. kitchen 10. accept

Activity 2 : Match the related sentences.

1. f 2. d 3. g 4. c 5. b 6. e 7. a

Activity 3 : Mixed-up Order Taking

	Drinks		Food items		
	Juice	Hot drink	1	2	3
Jeff	orange juice	coffee	toast	scrambled eggs	butter
Pierre	orange juice	chocolate	croissants	fruit yoghurt	butter
Susanna	orange juice	×	fried egg	sausages	mushroom
Helen	grapefruit	tea	croissants	butter	jam

| 저자 소개

한선희 교수는 경북여고 및 경북대학교 사범대학 영어교육과와 동 대학원을 졸업하고, 경희대학교에서 문학박사(영어학)를 취득하였다. 한국외국어대 영어과 강사를 거쳐 현재 대림대학교 호텔외식서비스과 교수로 재직하면서, 토익, 관광영어, 승무원영어, 레스토랑영어 등을 강의하고 있다.

[저서 및 논문]

- Prosody in Lexical Phonology: Cases in English and Korean
- Some Processes in Korean Phonology
- 한국어의 운율구조
- 한국어 운율경계의 음성-음향적 특질연구
- 대화체 억양구말 형태소의 경계성조 연구
- Writing Start
- Becoming Writers
- Traveler's English
- English for Cabin Crew and Travelers
- 하늘을 나는 영어
- 나는 키친 잉글리시다

등 다수

나는 레스토랑 영어다(I'm Restaurant English)

2017년 2월 28일 초　판 발행
2019년 2월 28일 2판 1쇄 발행
2021년 8월 20일 2판 2쇄 발행

저　자 한 선 희
발행인 한 인 환
발행처 도서출판 **기 문 사**
등　록 1978. 8. 9. NO. 6-0637
주　소 서울시 동대문구 안암로 50-1(용두동) 홍신빌딩 3층
전　화 02) 2265-7214 / 922-8662~8663
팩　스 02) 922-8772

homepage : www.kimoonsa.co.kr
e-mail : book@kimoonsa.co.kr

ISBN : 978-89-7723-818-3 93740

정가 : 15,000원

저자와의 협의하에 인지생략